Safety of Web Applications

Series Editor
Jean-Charles Pomerol

Safety of Web Applications

*Risks, Encryption and Handling
Vulnerabilities with PHP*

Éric Quinton

First published 2017 in Great Britain and the United States by ISTE Press Ltd and Elsevier Ltd

ISTE Press Ltd
27-37 St George's Road
London SW19 4EU
UK

www.iste.co.uk

Elsevier Ltd
The Boulevard, Langford Lane
Kidlington, Oxford, OX5 1GB
UK

www.elsevier.com

Notices

Knowledge and best practice in this field are constantly changing. As new research and experience broaden our understanding, changes in research methods, professional practices, or medical treatment may become necessary.

Practitioners and researchers must always rely on their own experience and knowledge in evaluating and using any information, methods, compounds, or experiments described herein. In using such information or methods they should be mindful of their own safety and the safety of others, including parties for whom they have a professional responsibility.

To the fullest extent of the law, neither the Publisher nor the authors, contributors, or editors, assume any liability for any injury and/or damage to persons or property as a matter of products liability, negligence or otherwise, or from any use or operation of any methods, products, instructions, or ideas contained in the material herein.

For information on all our publications visit our website at http://store.elsevier.com/

British Library Cataloguing-in-Publication Data
A CIP record for this book is available from the British Library
Library of Congress Cataloging in Publication Data
A catalog record for this book is available from the Library of Congress
ISBN 978-1-78548-228-1

Printed and bound in the UK and US

Contents

Preface

When I first began my career in the 1980s, personal computing was in its infancy. The first computers had very little internal memory, so files and even entire booting routines were stored on floppy disks with very low storage capacity. Graphical interfaces did not yet exist, or in some cases were just beginning to be introduced. To exchange information with other users, we used floppy disks, and more powerful computer systems used magnetic tapes. Mainframe computers were accessed by passive terminals connected together with dedicated cables (one cable per terminal). These were called *serial links*.

During the 1990s, as computing power increased, direct wired connections were gradually replaced by networks, and terminals were replaced by PCs. Computers then began to start dialoguing with each other internally, within companies. However, exchanges between different locations were limited, since communication costs were exorbitant and only very low bandwidths were possible. Applications were written for specific operating systems, which were in perfect control of their environments: all monitors had the same characteristics, as did all computers (PCs).

In the late 1990s, the development of the Internet and the creation of the first websites open to the general public profoundly changed the lay of the land. The shift from dedicated applications on specific devices to the more general form of web applications deeply disrupted approaches to programming. Now, anyone can connect to any software, access information, order products, manage their emails, and so on.

In the 2000s, with the proliferation of wireless connections (WiFi only really began to become widespread in France in the mid-2000s), the developer community also began to become aware of the security problems associated with this new environment. Before then, problems had been relatively well-isolated, since IT professionals were rare and also because systems enjoyed perfect control of their technical environments. This does not mean that security was completely neglected (encryption has always existed), but rather that, as a general rule, only companies or organizations that handled sensitive information (banks, military, etc.) paid any special attention to security. For most companies, the risk of data loss was very often the only factor taken into consideration, and even then only very loose protective measures were taken. The identify of users was also typically verified using unencrypted logins and passwords, since the risk of this information being intercepted was still relatively low. The available computer equipment was not yet powerful enough to implement "real-time" encryption anyway.

But individuals, and in some cases organizations, quickly realized the potential financial and later political advantages that could be obtained by targeting these web applications: the Internet was no longer static as in its early days (initially, web pages could not be modified), but had now become dynamic. Now, users themselves can request specific behavior from the server, and influence the information that is presented to them.

Web applications thus acquired a new dimension of risk: the information submitted by the browser needs to be systematically checked. Unanticipated behavior can occur if the user sends data specially modified with the objective of causing the server to react differently. This is, for example, the case with SQL injection, which, without the appropriate security measures, tricks the server into executing operations that were not planned by the programmer.

Today, web software development requires an extremely varied spectrum of skills (programming languages such as PHP, HTML for drawing pages, CSS for stylizing them uniquely, JavaScript and its extensions such as JQuery for building interactivity, SQL for accessing databases, etc.).

Many programmers learn these languages without necessarily being made aware of the risks to which they are exposed. Basic training rarely focuses on these aspects (with the exception of specialized training), or only addresses some of them, preferring to focus on more rudimentary skills. It is all too common to meet newly qualified developers with very little knowledge of how to secure their software. This is also often true with self-taught students, who learn to program to meet a specific need, such as setting up a website for an organization, or who write interfaces to control small databases.

Yet the risks are ever-present: without special protective measures, data can be corrupted, and the website can be used as a gateway by an attacker seeking to take control of the company information system, or might be defaced for politically motivated reasons.

Taking the time to examine the security of an application is therefore particularly important. The first step of this process is to perform risk assessment: a banking application is more sensitive than a system for booking meeting rooms.

The next step is to consider the runtime environment of the program. This might not be intrinsically safe: if the machines that host the application are not well protected themselves, any protective measures built into the code will be essentially useless. Similarly, exchanges between the server and users must be encrypted to prevent undesirable eavesdropping, or malicious modifications to the exchanged information performed in real time. Of course, these considerations begin to exceed the scope of just the program code, but one should note that encryption mechanisms are widely used by a large number of routines, in particular for the guarantees that they can provide for certain types of operation.

Understanding the risks to which the code is exposed is a complex topic, simply due to the sheer variety of the potential mechanisms by which it could be attacked. Fortunately, there exist projects such as OWASP that regularly publish lists of the most common types of attack, each of which can often be thwarted by a few lines of code. ANSSI, the French National Agency for Information Systems Security, also regularly publishes advice and risk analysis methodology in the form of the EBIOS method.

One important aspect of security is managing users and their access rights. Several different mechanisms can be used to identify users and allow them to access the information that they need.

Designing an application is a complex task, and the only way to ensure that security measures are correctly applied everywhere is to structure the code accordingly. Organizational methods, such as the MVC model (model, view, controller), can be used to fulfill these needs, and ensure that the application operates both reliably and securely.

Finally, testing the developed software with special tools will allow us to identify the most obvious shortcomings. This is an important step before beginning production, and provides users with a guarantee that the necessary precautions have been taken to anticipate risks.

This book presents a large number of examples. Most of them are written in PHP, which is one of the most common languages for creating web applications. These examples can of course be adapted to fit other languages. Often, only a few lines of code is required to patch a vulnerability, and the algorithm or approach used to tackle the problem is more interesting than the actual code itself.

Éric QUINTON

February 2017

1

Why Do Web Applications
Need to be Secure?

1.1. What is a web application?

An *application*, or *program*, may be defined as a set of instructions that can be interpreted by a computer system, involving data. A *web application* is a program whose user interface runs in the browser, and whose logic is processed by a server, i.e. a remote machine. The browser and the server communicate over a network, the *web* – a collection of computer equipment and cables that allows information to be exchanged, and a protocol, the *Internet*.

1.1.1. *The Internet, a global network*

The Internet is a protocol for exchanging messages between computers whose earliest foundations date back to the 1960s, but which first became truly operational in the 1980s. Each machine was originally identified by a unique address called an IP address (Internet Protocol), based on the principle that any computer should be able to communicate with any other. If we were to draw a diagram of the connections between all of the devices, it would look like a gigantic spiderweb – hence, the name web.

The Internet is a network: the services built on top of it are what makes it special. The Internet allows messages to be exchanged via email, direct discussions to be held via forum protocols (most popular in the 1990s), and, of course, information to be viewed on the user's screen due to the HTTP protocol. The primary reason that this protocol was developed is that it allows users to navigate from one piece of information to the next in no specific order, using hyperlinks – this is known as surfing.

To make navigating easier, the original IP addresses were replaced with names that are easier to remember. In practice, IP addresses still exist, but translation servers Domain Name Service (DNS) are used to perform the conversion.

Most websites begin with the famous three letters World Wide Web (WWW). This term encompasses all servers that provide information viewed through browsers, which are programs installed on user devices that allow webpages to be displayed.

The current version of the web dates back to the early 1990s. This is when the HTML format was invented for designing webpages. At the time, however, the concept of web application was not yet familiar.

1.1.2. *Programs before the web*

Before the World Wide Web, programs were generated differently according to system on which they were intended to run: a program running on a Macintosh computer could not be used with another computer with a different operating system – the program that controls the computer – such as Windows. Programmers were faced with a difficult problem: how could they write an application that can run on all systems?

In the late 1990s, the company Sun (which has since been acquired by Oracle) gave the first answer to this question by creating Java. Java is based on two building blocks: a programming language and an execution layer programmed specifically for each operating system.

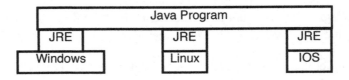

Figure 1.1. *Working principle of Java applications*

Any program written in Java can be run on any platform with the execution layer, the Java Runtime Environment (JRE), without requiring the code to be recompiled. The main drawback is that the JRE must be installed on each computer that runs the application. The program itself must also be distributed to each user and installed on each computer. Clearly, this solution is not yet completely ideal.

1.1.3. Web technology is gradually adopted by applications

IT professionals soon realized how powerful the web could become. To create programs, we can simply run a piece of code on the server that generates the pages dynamically, depending on what the user wishes to see. Any browser can operate this program, no matter where it is hosted, so long as the user has an Internet connection.

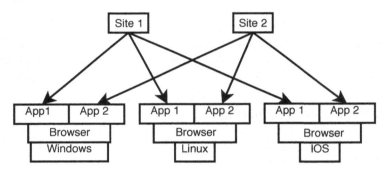

Figure 1.2. *Working principle of web applications*

Each computer has its own operating system (*Windows*, *Linux*, or *IOS* in this example). One specific program, the browser, is installed on each device: it can display any page returned by a website. If this page is created dynamically, that is to say, if it is recalculated by the website server each time that it is requested to adapt it to each request submitted by the user, we describe it as a *web application*. In this case, the server generates pages using a suitable language.

Historically, PHP was one of the first languages to be used, but since then, there have been others, such as Python and Java.

In the early 2000s, HTML could not rival the performance of programs written specifically for each operating system, or developed in Java (or other languages working according to similar principles).

Since then, it has vastly improved (we are currently using version 5), and we can now program actions to execute directly in the browser, for example by using the JavaScript language. Note that JavaScript has nothing to with Java, except for a certain similarity in the syntax and in the name.

Today, applications written using web technologies are no longer inferior to those developed specifically for a given operating system in most respects. They can be executed in the browser, regardless of the system that drives the browser, and boast a wide range of features.

However, one problem was soon discovered: the technologies that allow computers to communicate, which are sometimes described as the *network layer*, were not designed to be secure. The original designers mainly focused on the reliability of transmissions: the primary objective was to ensure that the messages exchanged between computers arrive safely at their destinations. At the time, very few people cared about guaranteeing confidentiality, and computers were not yet powerful enough to offer real-time encryption in the form that we are familiar with today.

1.1.4. *Exchange is based on trust*

Fundamentally, the Internet is not secure: without complementing it with other technologies, everybody can listen to the information being exchanged, or even modify it in real time.

Although this is generally not too much of a problem when viewing general information, it becomes an issue when updating databases, operating machinery and paying taxes: some level of confidentiality is necessary for these tasks. Today's web only works because it relies on trust.

For example, when we buy a product from a website, we must first trust the seller: we trust that the product that they are offering is available, and we trust that it will be delivered. The seller also needs to be sure that the delivery address given by the customer cannot be modified, etc. As for the payment, providing the credit card number is always tricky: the seller, or the bank acting as an intermediary for the seller, must guarantee both the confidentiality of the exchange and the security of the collected data.

This trust is an essential concept: although it was not fully necessary in primitive societies (as everybody could keep an eye on the whole community), this is no longer true today, since we need to conduct trades without knowing the other party personally. The need for security when interacting with others is indispensable, and relies not just on legal protective measures and regulations (the fact that companies must register on the Trade Registry, the risks involved with fraud, etc.), but also on the security processes in place to ensure that a third party cannot interfere with an interaction.

To close the security gaps (everything is open and accessible by default), a number of technical solutions have been implemented to provide secure access to servers, encrypt connections, and ensure that data cannot be intercepted.

It has also proven necessary to protect users themselves from information theft: if no special precautions are taken, a program provided by a server can easily access data on the user's computer and steal information.

To counter this, browser publishers have implemented a large array of security measures, for example by preventing webpages from accessing information on the user's computer. This is the main limitation of web applications: they are forbidden from interacting directly with the device.

Smartphones and tablets can circumvent this limitation, at the cost of requiring the application to be specially encapsulated. Today, these devices have a wide range of features, such as GPSes, cameras, accelerometers (which record movements and are, in particular, used to automatically rotate the screen), etc. To create an application that exploits these features using web technologies, multiple different languages are used, such as HTML, to prepare the displayed pages, and JavaScript, to manage the interactions with the device. The pages (the program) thus created are then encapsulated with special tools that make them usable. In this phase, access rights are granted to the finished application, which requests access to the hardware. To install these programs, virtual stores hosted by the operating system publishers (*Google Play Store* for Android, for example) act as an intermediate step, guaranteeing that the programs do not contain any malicious code that might compromise the system security.

1.1.5. *Bad idea: trusting that the intranet is automatically secure*

It might seem tempting to treat applications obtained directly from the Internet differently from those that only run internally (within the intranet of an organization). Although the risks are of course much higher with Internet applications, which are directly accessible by everyone in the world, we must not forget that even trusted personnel can behave inappropriately and attempt to modify information, whether for their own benefit or to harm the company for which they work.

Furthermore, many modern attacks work by taking control of one computer, which is then used as a springboard to assault other devices until, step by step, a server containing confidential information is reached.

While it is relatively natural to remember to secure an open web application downloaded from the Internet, it also makes sense to do the same for software that was not necessarily designed to be deployed outside of the company setting. Indeed, if, for whatever reason, it is made available at a later point in time, doing so will require fewer modifications, which will usually be limited to configuring the required network infrastructure. If security is not integrated into the design from the beginning, it will be much more complicated to implement later, and the effort required to develop additional protection modules can quickly become prohibitive.

1.2. What is computer security?

The proliferation of computers and the Internet means that we need to store and retrieve information from digital media on a daily basis, as well as perform operations controlled by computers.

If I want to make a bank transfer, I need the bank website to work, to display the correct information (the accuracy of my bank balance is important to me!), and I need to know that nobody else can access this information without my permission, or complete a transaction without my knowledge.

This example shows the three criteria required for me to trust my bank. First, *availability*: does the website always work when I need it to, and can I perform the transactions that I want, when I want? Second, *confidentiality*: am I the only person that can check my balance, with the exception of properly authorized bank personnel? Finally, *integrity*: is the information provided accurate and complete?

Securing an application or a website consists of implementing mechanisms that will allow users to place some level of trust in the host's ability to guarantee certain standards of confidentiality, availability and integrity.

1.2.1. *Security relies on many different blocks*

Contrary to what one might think at first glance, the security of a web application does not only depend on its code, but also on several other factors, such as the server, the network architecture, etc.

Today, the only device that is considered to be intrinsically safe is the smart card (at least in terms of data integrity and confidentiality – it can still be lost or destroyed): it does not require any other device to guarantee that it is secure. In every other case, several different blocks must collaborate to ensure that an application is protected.

Below is a diagram showing an example of a fairly standard technical architecture used for web platforms:

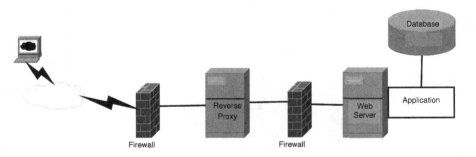

Figure 1.3. *The different building blocks required to access a web application over the Internet*

Consider a workstation equipped with a browser that connects to the Internet in order to access an application. It sends a request that is immediately processed by an initial firewall: a system that blocks all incoming connections unless they are authorized. In the case shown in the figure, the firewall only allows requests relating to access to the web server.

Once the request has passed through the firewall, it is handled by a dedicated server, the *reverse proxy*. This is a web server that simply modifies the destination address of the request and performs a few additional checks to ensure that the user does not know anything about the server that receives the request. This is often the level at which measures are taken to protect against attacks designed to saturate a machine, also known as *Denial of Service attacks* or DoS (see section 3.5.3).

A second firewall is then set up, which regulates access to the local network. Only connections originating from the reverse proxy server and headed toward the web server are allowed through. This firewall is often part of the web server, in the form of a program that filters connections originating from the network.

The web server hosts the application, which processes the submitted request. If necessary, the application queries the database to retrieve or store any information that it might need.

Each system plays a part in the overall security of the application. Depending on their roles, they influence either the confidentiality, availability or integrity.

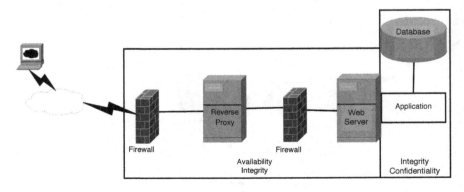

Figure 1.4. *The different blocks that participate in the security of the application*

The hardware primarily acts to meet the need for availability: if a machine experiences a failure, the application will cease to be accessible. The integrity-related protections provided by this level are most closely linked to loss of data: the technical mechanisms that are implemented must ensure that no information is lost by maintaining backups, system redundancy, etc.

The application itself must guarantee confidentiality, and to a lesser extent data integrity, in particular to ensure that attackers cannot modify information without authorization.

Thus, to secure an application, we must not only consider the actual code, but also its execution environment.

1.2.2. *Not all applications are equal in terms of security needs*

I do not need all applications to guarantee the same level of security: although inconsistencies in my bank statements would be unacceptable to me, I would probably not care too much about an unavailable or erroneous weather forecast, unless my activities that day are closely linked to the weather.

Implementing security mechanisms costs time and money. For example, in order to guarantee that a program will be operational 24 hours a day, a backup server room is likely necessary, in case the primary server room experiences an incident (power outage, fire, etc.). In vital industry sectors, these rooms need to be sufficiently distant from each other that if the whole facility is destroyed, for example by a natural disaster or an industrial accident, the backup server room still remains unaffected. The cost of communicating between these two rooms will probably be higher if they are more than a few kilometers apart, and will require lines to be leased from operators.

There are several methods for defining the required security level. Some methods use reasoning based on the availability, i.e. the hardware chain on which the application runs. In which case, the companies would study and implement a *business continuity plan*. This plan takes local factors into account (is the company located in a flood zone, or near a high-risk establishment?) as well as the security objectives.

For the program, the security study attempts to define the expectations in terms of confidentiality, integrity and availability (this information must be consistent with the business continuity plan). The risk posed to the business by any possible source of failure is evaluated.

This is used to define the level of security that must be met by the future application: does it just need to be capable of resisting opportunistic attacks, i.e. randomly conducted attacks? Or does it need to be resistant to attacks that target it specifically? Is the risk sufficiently high that every possible measure must be taken to ensure maximal robustness?

We will begin by studying the concepts used by business continuity plans, and we also continue to discuss how to evaluate the security level required by a program.

1.3. Examples of damage caused by security failures

Thirty years ago, when I first started my career, computer security was scarce. Although the first viruses had already begun to bother us, they could only propagate via floppy disks (which had a storage capacity of 1.44 Mb!), so they were not a major concern.

Furthermore, very few people knew anything about computers: security by obscurity! In the 1990s, I came across examples of important applications used to pay subsidies whose main administrative account for the database was not even password-protected! But since networks and the Internet did not yet exist, there was limited risk, and only few IT professionals were capable of system penetration.

Today, the situation is radically different. Due to state-sponsored and corporate espionage parties with malicious intent, etc., coupled with a network that is available everywhere and a certain impunity originating from the architecture of the Internet network itself, not to mention the fact that large parts of the population are skilled in computer technologies, attacks have now become commonplace.

Implementing a new application is often necessary or even critical for business activities in today's competitive environment. However, applications can also cause problems if their security is compromised: financial losses, time, reputation and legal repercussions are examples of the possible cost of failure.

A few years ago, there was a Dutch company in the business of providing digital certificates, most notably used by the HTTPS protocol for encrypting traffic between browsers and web servers.

The HTTPS protocol, as we will see in section 3.4, uses two keys: a public key (the digital certificate) and a private key, which must be kept secret. The public key is signed by a certificate authority: if this authority accidentally reveals the private key used to sign certificates, anybody can generate them, and website owners can no longer be reliably authenticated.

This company was targeted by a cyber-attack, and its root certificate (the private key) was stolen: the hackers were therefore able to generate as many certificates as they wanted, allowing them to easily intercept traffic and generate false certificates to mislead users.

The root certificate was very quickly revoked and deleted from users' browsers. Consequently, all other certificates that it had been used to generate were also revoked. The company had to declare bankruptcy [WIK 15c]: the cyber-attack led to its ruin.

Not every example is this serious, but the consequences can nevertheless be significant. It shows that the risks must be taken into consideration from the earliest stages of the project.

In recent years, shop cash registers have been automated, i.e. operated by a remote server. Imagine what would happen if the computer system fails on the Saturday afternoon before Christmas: it would not be possible to record any payments. Clearly, this risk must be considered by the analysis: the loss of revenue would largely cover the costs of implementing a backup solution.

In a similar spirit, many companies save credit card numbers – not just banks, but also large Internet-based traders, such as *Amazon* and *Google*.

Although there are many advantages for companies in having the card payment information of their customers (purchasing is faster and encouraging more impulsive buying), this requires trust. If a website accidentally reveals the payment information of its customers, there is a good chance that they will want to switch providers. Unfortunately, this kind of incident does in fact happen on a regular basis, even to banks and the companies that issue cards on their behalf [LEM 14].

Similarly, if an attacker manages to modify the details of an order, for example by changing the shipping address of the items ordered by customers to an arbitrary location, they will be able to cause significant damage, both to the company's finances and reputation. It is highly unlikely that a customer that has been duped in this way will wish to return to the same website to place another order.

In the same way, we should not make the mistake of believing that confidential applications are safe from these kinds of attempt.

Imagine a research laboratory that develops an application for data entry. If this application is poorly designed, it can, in some cases, allow code to be executed directly on the server that hosts it. If an attacker manages to corrupt the way that it normally operates, they can infiltrate the server, from where it is highly likely that they will be able to access the full information system of the laboratory, allowing them to search for more valuable information.

Just because some access paths are well protected (this is often the case for network interconnection equipment in the world wide web) it does not mean that their content is fully inaccessible. A five-meter-high wall is not much use if a door is accidentally left open, or if it is only secured by a simple latch that can easily be opened from the inside. Anybody with access to the door can leave it open: this is what can happen if an attacker manages to take control of a server or an internal computer system.

Sometimes, the stakes are high enough that attackers are willing to spend vast resources to penetrate a system. You might, for example, remember the incident suffered by the Iranian states a few years ago. Iran was attempting to enrich uranium to produce enough material to make an atomic bomb. This enrichment was performed by a centrifuge system: since uranium isotopes have different masses, the centrifuge can separate the minerals by causing the heavier elements to move outward. A particularly well-designed cyber-attack [BEN 10] destroyed the centrifuges by making them spin too rapidly. It probably required months of preparation by exceptionally competent teams. Experts estimated that this attack set the Iranian nuclear program back by at least 1 year, which was enough to change the direction of their national policy and facilitate subsequent negotiations.

Similarly, international politics can change extremely quickly, and a company or an organization that seems unexposed can very quickly find themselves in the spotlight, targeted by a coordinated retaliatory attack.

Although there are many different possible vectors for an attack, searching for flaws in web software is often one of the simplest routes. If an application is poorly protected and an attacker manages to modify its usual behavior so that it allows them to install a malicious program on the server, they will be able to target other components of the company's information system.

Many security experts no longer ask: *Can this system be attacked?* but rather: *When will it be attacked?* This does not mean that we should give in to paranoia: the risk should be studied, and there are always ways to make life difficult for any would-be attackers. But we should remember that no system is impenetrable, even though some systems are more difficult to beat than others.

1.3.1. *Do not take anything for granted*

Security is a lesson in modesty: no matter what you do, some clever attacker will be able to find a way to bypass it. Applications that seemed reliable 10 years ago can be easy to hack today.

Over the last few years, attacks have become increasingly sophisticated. It is not uncommon for attackers to work for several months to prepare an attack, devoting substantial human and financial resources to their task. This is far from the mental image of a brilliant teenager bringing government institutions to their knees! Of course, the attack needs to be "worthwhile" relative to the invested resources.

But even with applications that are not highly critical, the risk is never zero: opportunistic attacks can, for example, be mounted on websites that rely on a shared framework using newly discovered security vulnerabilities. It is easy for attackers to exploit these kinds of vulnerability, allowing them to access valuable information or gain access to other components that theoretically should have been better protected. For example, many websites are built with the WordPress publishing engine [WOR 15], one of the most popular content management systems.

A serious vulnerability was discovered in 2014 [ZDN 14]: all websites using this engine became vulnerable to attack. As it always takes some time for vulnerabilities to be patched (they require an update, which can take time, especially if the website is not managed by IT teams with experience in this kind of task), attackers can randomly launch attacks, hoping to stumble upon an unprotected website.

After penetrating the system, they can publish a political message, or attempt to directly access the computer and find information that they can monetize.

1.3.2. *Well-structured applications are easier to secure*

There is always something that we can do to limit the risk. The first step is to define the security level required by the application. Display websites that present a company and only contain general information (industry sector, services offered) are not as sensitive as sales websites or payroll management systems.

If the architecture of the application is properly designed, it will be easier to implement additional security checks. For example, we can rely on models designed according to the MVC paradigm (*model – view – controller*). One particular aspect of this model is its unique controller (or a single family of controllers inheriting from this unique controller), which serves as a gateway (see Chapter 6). Similarly, data are sent to the browser using *views*[1]: any checks or formatting implemented in these views is performed once for each output.

The model itself (and in particular the part of the model that accesses the database) is also based on a single object responsible for guaranteeing that information remains secure.

If there is no single gateway, implementing any additional security functions requires each page to be updated one by one. Not only does this quickly become tedious, but individual pages might be omitted, or mistakes might accidentally be introduced into the code.

---

1 There can be multiple types of view, depending on the nature of the information to be transmitted: webpages, but also JSON files in response to an AJAX request, CSV files, PDF files, etc.

When I performed the security review of one of my most recent applications using the documents published by Open Web Application Security Project (OWASP) [OWA 15a], which we will encounter later), I found a vulnerability that I was not previously aware of. My application expected UTF-8 encoding, which could be exploited by certain types of attack to execute malicious code. The solution is to check that any input data are indeed encoded with UTF-8 . In fact, there is a simple PHP function that performs this check. Closing the security gap was as simple as adding 20 or so lines of code to the beginning of the controller code (see section 4.3.1).

Thus, I was able to protect the entirety of my application against an unanticipated type of attack simply by modifying a single file, the controller.

1.3.3. *The only type of security that matters is global security*

Except for smart cards, which are intrinsically secure (their security does not depend on third-party mechanisms, as we mentioned earlier), a computer system can only be considered secure if it is implemented within certain conditions. Imagine an application equipped with the latest state-of-the-art security measures. If it is deployed on a server that is left completely open, all of these security measures will be essentially useless: illegitimate access to the server will allow attackers to circumvent all protective measures.

We will discuss how to implement a certain number of security measures in web applications, but we will also discuss how the servers themselves must be configured. This will allow us to define rules that should be applied during production, and to clarify the general context that needs to be available before we can consider an application to be reasonably secure relative to the chosen objectives.

These rules are not a replacement for the work performed by network architects to properly protect servers and local networks: layers are often added to make things more difficult for attackers, such as firewalls that block some types of attack, antiviruses installed on the network equipment and proxies that allow servers to work through indirect connections to the world wide web, etc.

Of course, it is rarely the responsibility of the developer to implement these protective measures. But it may be fruitful to open a dialogue with technical teams to discover whether certain checks are already provided by the platform, to avoid having to include them in the application code. This is especially true for some aspects that relate to changes in the web server configuration, which might be performed either globally or application by application.

1.3.4. *What security measures are required by applications with heavy clients?*

All too often, people only examine the security of web applications. One might be tempted to think that applications executed entirely from within a workstation are unlikely to be attacked from the outside.

However, this is not the case. Applications handle information, and this information is probably valuable to the company. If a database is used by an application, and this database runs on the computer, it might potentially be accessed by other applications. Indeed, by default, local databases are not password-protected, since they are not accessible from the computer network; but a malicious program downloaded from a website might also attempt to access this database. This is in fact a common mechanism for attacking smartphones.

Furthermore, it is likely the case that the data handled by the PC will be transferred to the company information system: how is this transfer conducted?

Finally, laptops are easily stolen while traveling. If confidential data are not properly protected, this can quickly cause problems.

Today, these risks are exacerbated by smartphones, which run all kinds of applications. Before developing software for this type of platform, good practice dictates that we should first consult the documents published by OWASP [OWA 15a], which describe the checks that should be made, depending on the sensitivity of the application. There are sections dedicated to these platforms.

Thus, even for applications with heavy clients, it is advisable to conduct a security assessment, and if necessary to implement the appropriate protective measures. This is true on every operating system, whether Android, Windows, Linux or IOS: if a target is considered to be significant in some way, attackers will be prepared to develop specialized attacks, even for less common platforms.

We will not particularly focus on this aspect of security: one should simply remember that care is required when storing sensitive information (login details, credit card numbers, etc.), that developing robust login strategies for embedded databases is preferable (whenever applicable) and that in many cases the very first measure that should be taken is to encrypt the storage medium.

We must bear in mind that there is always a potential risk, and that this risk must be estimated: this will allow us to develop a solution that is appropriate for our needs.

2

Estimating Risk

2.1. What is risk?

Risk is a relatively elusive concept. It can be expressed as the combination of the possibility of an event, a target and an impact.

Consider an example from everyday life. If someone drives too fast on a mountain road, they risk crashing, which would result in some degree of damage or injury.

The event associated with the risk is the crash, which represents the consequence of speeding. Together, these two points form a scenario, i.e. a series of necessary prerequisites for the accident to occur. The probability of the event depends on the driving speed, road and weather conditions, traffic, etc. The target is the car and the people inside, as well as any external objects involved in the accident (property, passers-by, etc.). Finally, the impact is the result of the damage caused, which can range from mild (a few scratches on the body of the car) to serious (death or hospitalization of a person).

Thus, we can represent the risk in terms of these four factors: the cause or the scenario, the probability of occurrence, the target and the impact (Figure 2.1).

This model can easily be adapted to describe the potential damage to an information system, for example due to an insecure web application.

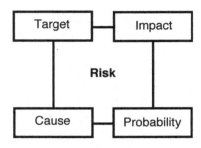

Figure 2.1. *Risk*

2.2. How can we protect ourselves from risk?

Once the risk has been identified, there are several possible strategies for preventing it from materializing, or for mitigating its impact. Returning to our example of mountain driving, there are multiple possible approaches. The first is to avoid driving in the mountains, and to choose safer roads, which might, however, increase the length of the voyage. We could also equip the car with specialized tires (e.g. snow tires in winter), and ensure that all passengers fasten their seatbelts. Finally, driving carefully, at a controlled speed, is another way of providing security.

The EBIOS method[1] proposes four strategies for managing risks: avoidance, reduction, transfer or acceptance.

Avoidance consists of selecting an option that renders the event improbable, for example taking the highway or canceling the trip. In terms of computer systems, this might correspond to the decision to avoid computerizing a procedure if the risk for the company is disproportionate to the expected benefits.

Reduction involves implementing measures to limit either the probability or the impact of the risk (snow tires, seatbelt, controlled speed, etc.). In

---

1 There are several global methods for defining the computer security requirements of a company. In France, two methods are predominantly used (but others exist): MEHARI [CLU 15a], proposed by CLUSIF, the French Information Security Club [CLU 15b] and EBIOS [ANS 10], proposed by ANSSI, the National Agency for Information Systems Security [ANS 15]. These methods restate or comply with the international ISO norms for risk management [ISO 09, ISO 11, ISO 15].

development projects, this includes most of the implemented security measures, as well as data backup mechanisms, for example.

Transfer consists of asking a third party to assume responsibility for the risk. Thus, instead of driving a car, we could decide to travel by bus: the transportation company and their driver will instead be responsible for the risk. Of course, we do not have to choose the tour operator at random; we can base our decision on objective information (regulations, company reputation, etc.). For computer systems, choosing a web host that guarantees 24/7 availability falls into this category. Similarly, another example is when an SME sends a copy of its data to a service provider offering a cloud-based product: the data are entrusted to a third party with the facilities and servers to adequately protect against loss. Again, the choice of provider and the contract between both parties is not left to chance, and it is important to verify beforehand that the third party will be capable of effectively fulfilling the responsibility that is transferred to them.

Finally, accepting the risk in its current form may be a viable choice. For example, a program used to book meeting rooms in a company can afford to be somewhat unprotected: if information is lost or corrupted, the risk of disruption is small. But this option can only be taken as part of an informed decision, and must not be the default course of action: if problems do arise, the absence of decision would be blamed on the person who had implemented the project.

2.3. Determining the target

Consider once again the diagram showing a typical example of the technical architecture behind a web application (Figure 2.2).

Two potential targets are shown. The target on the left largely concerns aspects relating to the network, server operation and safeguards against intrusion. It is relevant when drafting a business continuity plan, and when studying the risk associated with network infrastructure.

The second, on the right, corresponds to our web application project. It includes software components corresponding to the web server, the application itself and the database.

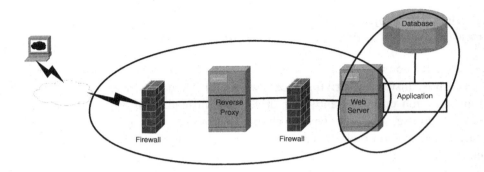

Figure 2.2. *Determining the target*

The target can be refined depending on the maturity of the company. If security measures are already in place and operational at the web server level, they do not need to be re-examined by the study. Similarly, if the database server is fully protected, and specific procedures are imposed on the developers, then this aspect does not need to be included either.

The choice of target is particularly important: if chosen too small, it is highly likely that security gaps will slip through. If too large, the study will become more complex, and redundant security measures might be proposed, which cost time and money.

Typically, risk analysis for IT development projects is limited to the web server, or at least the implementation of the application within this server, the program itself and its connections with the database(s).

2.4. Determining the impact

This is probably the most complicated component of risk analysis (we will see that the scenario analysis can be transferred).

The impact is determined in two steps. First, the security needs are estimated, and then the impact of failure is evaluated.

The security needs are usually determined according to three criteria, also known as CIA (from the first letter of each criterion): confidentiality, integrity and availability. The criteria are usually graded from 1 to 4, where 1 is the lowest level of need and 4 is the highest level.

These assessment grids are filled out by the company, which adapts them to their environment and effective needs. Example grids are of course available; a few examples are presented below, and others are available from ANSSI [ANS 10].

2.4.1. *Confidentiality*

Confidentiality aims to determine who should have access to information. Some information is public, such as messages posted on a forum: anybody can read it. However, customer bank details, personal information protected by data protection legislation and connection details (login and password) could cause devastating damage if they are leaked. For example, when attackers were able to obtain login information from extramarital dating websites [ITE 15]: the impact was disastrous for the company that failed to properly protect its data.

Below Table 2.1 is an example of a confidentiality assessment grid.

Level	Description
1. Public	Information accessible to all
2. Limited	Information only accessible to employees and partners
3. Reserved	Information only accessible to the relevant internal employees
4. Private	Information only accessible to identified individuals who need access to it

Table 2.1. *Level definitions for the confidentiality scale*

Level 1 corresponds to general information, such as the information published on public websites. Level 2 usually corresponds to the information handled by administrative applications. Individuals with access can manipulate this information with no special restrictions.

Level 3 is applicable to personal data, such as bank transactions and balances. This should only be accessible to the individuals to whom it relates (in this example, the bank customers) and personnel authorized to view or change the data. Furthermore, customers should not be able to view information that is not theirs.

Finally, in this context, level 4 corresponds to data that should not be accessed or changed except by personnel who actually require access to it, regardless of their credentials or hierarchical position. This principle is used to manage classified military information.

Up to level 3, access can be managed by the application itself. At level 4, complex encryption and permissions procedures and possibly computer network isolation protocols are likely to be necessary.

2.4.2. *Integrity*

Integrity defines whether it is acceptable for information to be corrupted or lost, and the required conditions for restoring data.

This criterion combines two different aspects. The first relates to the loss of information: a server failure or a mistake can cause data to be lost. In the best-case scenario, it will be possible to recover to an intact previous state, if backups are available and can be used for restoration, or if the database is configured to track all operations (for example using application logging techniques or by synchronizing between servers).

In this respect, integrity primarily consists of defining acceptable time periods for data loss.

It would be unacceptable for a bank transaction to be lost, due to the economic significance of each transaction. However, it is acceptable for an office file to be lost if an earlier, fairly recent version can be recovered. Classical backup systems work with *time steps* of half-days or days, which is often sufficient. Losing a file is never pleasant, but in many cases reconstructing it is relatively easy, although this of course takes time and creates frustration.

This criterion is evaluated by choosing the *maximum admissible data loss*, which will in particular determine the technical environment required by the application (database synchronization for remote environments, backup policies, etc.).

The second aspect relates to the corruption of information: corrupted information is still present, but has been modified, either unintentionally by a computer error or an erroneous operation or voluntarily by a deliberate act. In some cases, this may not be serious, as it may be possible to revert to a previous state, for example using backups. In other cases, it may pose more of a problem, for example in the case of bank transactions or legal documents. In these cases, the application must incorporate mechanisms for guaranteeing the integrity of information, either by redundant self-checking systems, or by signing the data to guarantee that it has not been modified.

Table 2.2 provides an example of an integrity scale.

Level	Description
1. Modifiable	The information being processed does not require integrity; the data may be modified without significant consequences
2. Detectable	The information does not require integrity, provided that modifications are identifiable and it is possible to revert to a previous state if necessary by restoring from a backup
3. Controlled	The information does not require integrity, provided that modifications are tracked and the information is retrievable; it is essential to monitor all modifications in real time (full logging procedures to track all changes)
4. Signed	The information requires strict integrity in all circumstances, if necessary by an electronic signing or encryption procedure

Table 2.2. *Level definitions for the integrity scale*

Level 1 of this scale is rarely applicable. It could for example apply to internal applications whose content becomes irrelevant once it has been generated, such as the results of calculations that can be repeated. This describes any information that can be deleted without causing damage.

Level 2 corresponds to systems with regular backup procedures. We can always revert to the previous state by restoring data from other media (for example laboratory notebooks).

Level 3 does not allow any loss of information: database replication procedures, tracking logs, etc., are mandatory. This is typically the level required for banking transactions or just-in-time processes.

Level 4 is more restrictive: the information may not be modified once it has been validated. For example, the Chamber of French Notaries [NOT 15] has developed an application that allows notarized documents to be electronically signed. Once they have been signed, they cannot be modified. The architecture for implementing this is much more complex and relies on archiving and electronic signing technologies.

2.4.3. *Availability*

Availability defines the period during which it is acceptable for the data, or the application, to be inaccessible. If the application for booking meeting rooms stops working for a few days, it will nevertheless be possible to revert to manual scheduling in the interim. But supermarket cash registers cannot afford interruptions of more than a few seconds or minutes.

Table 2.3 provides an example of an availability scale.

Level	Description
1. More than 72 h	The application can be unavailable for more than 72 h
2. Between 24 and 72 h	The application must restore availability within 3 days
3. Between 4 and 24 h	The application must restore availability within 24 h
4. < 4 h	The application must restore availability within 4 h

Table 2.3. *Level definitions for the availability scale*

The choice of availability requirements will directly affect the cost of the solution that is ultimately implemented. Three days is plenty of time for an interruption to be resolved (this is enough time to reinstall the server and restore the data), but as the target recovery period becomes shorter, guaranteeing availability becomes increasingly complex to achieve.

If the target is to restore availability within less than 1 day, a backup platform is required, ready to be activated in the event of an incident. An administrator is also needed to monitor this platform and make the necessary arrangements.

To restore availability within half of a day, the recovery mechanisms need to be automated, and data need to be synchronized between the production platform and backup platform. And if no downtime whatsoever is acceptable, high-availability mechanisms distributed over at least two different facilities are required to limit the risk of failure in one of these facilities (for example network or power outage). An increased number of staff is also required to manage this infrastructure.

Therefore, determining the appropriate level of availability will strongly affect the total cost of the project and the complexity of its implementation.

2.4.4. *Determining the level of risk associated with a project*

In the previous section, we discussed requirements in terms of availability, integrity and confidentiality. For each of these criteria, it is important to estimate the damage that could be caused if an incident occurs. For example, what would happen if the cash registers stop working for longer than 10 min?

The risk is usually estimated using a four-level scale.

Table 2.4 shows the examples given in the EBIOS method.

Level	Description
1. Negligible	The impact will be overcome with no difficulty
2. Limited	The impact will be overcome with some difficulty
3. High	The impact will be overcome, but with serious difficulties
4. Critical	The impact cannot be overcome, and the survival of the company is threatened

Table 2.4. *List of risk levels*

These risk levels are not assessed globally, but are usually structured into four categories: internal disruption, financial losses, company reputation and liability commitments (or legal risk).

Internal disruption includes everything that relates to everyday business activities: this could range from delays in processing files to fundamental disarray, social movements, etc.

The financial loss is the amount of money required to restore the systems after a failure, either in terms of revenue lost due to the failure, or expenditure required following third-party proceedings (financial penalties, court judgments, damages and interest, etc.).

The activities of any company rely heavily on their reputation with their customers. If a major software program (for example a web-based sales application) does not work or leaks confidential information, the company's reputation and customer trust might be seriously compromised, which could jeopardize the future of the company.

Finally, if the company is left open to legal proceedings following a security breach, in particular if contractual clauses had been drawn or the latest standards had not been complied with, the impact may be significant, resulting in high financial losses, high workloads, reputation losses, etc.

After defining each of the criteria and establishing the impact table, one last important task still remains: defining the potential impact of failure for each criterion.

The following summary Table 2.5 can be used.

Criterion	Required level	Internal	Financial	Liability	Reputation	Max. impact
Confidentiality						
Integrity						
Availability						

Table 2.5. *Assessment table for the impact of failure*

The first column indicates the target level for each criterion. The estimated impact of failure is listed in each of the next four columns for each risk category. Finally, the last column summarizes the maximum risk exposure for that criterion.

Crucially, the impact must be estimated at the level of the company itself, and not at the level of the software requester or their department. Indeed, when a security vulnerability is discovered, the company itself is called into question, not just its IT, financial or sales departments. This key distinction must be kept in mind: individuals will always tend to maximize any risks that concern them directly, due to the impact that they could have on their own career within the company.

Imagine an incident that could cause internal users to lose confidence in a service. The software requester will likely estimate the level of risk to be fairly high, at 3 or 4. However, at the level of the company, the actual risk might be much lower: it might prove necessary to reorganize a few services, which could indeed be a complicated task, or alternatively an employee may need to be dismissed or transferred, etc., but none of this would prevent the company from continuing to operate as usual.

It is important to remember this nuance when performing risk analysis. Establishing an appropriate estimate that relates to the actual risk for the company will often avoid unnecessarily implementing heavy and expensive security procedures. Conversely, if a major risk is identified, it should be escalated to management, who must then decide whether the advantages of computerizing the procedure justify the associated risk, or authorize the appropriate resources to contain or handle this risk.

2.5. Which causes or scenarios should be considered?

We have now estimated the impact of an information system failure from the perspective of the company. But, to protect ourselves, we still need to know what the potential threats might be.

When establishing a business continuity plan, it is relatively easy to list all possible causes of failure: human risk, power or network outage, technological risk (facilities classified as being potentially dangerous), natural risk (flooding, earthquakes, fire, etc.) and so on.

In the case of computer applications, this exercise becomes much more difficult. Although it is relatively easy to anticipate hardware failures (which should in principle be included in the business continuity plan), strictly cyber-based attack scenarios are much more difficult to enumerate.

IT, and software development in particular, is an example of immaterial technology. This means that making programs work is not a mechanical process – designing these programs is an intellectual activity that heavily relies on the imagination. If two developers are given the same task without any particular restrictions, they will develop significantly different programs, both in terms of user-oriented approach and internal design.

Cyber-attacks are also the fruit of the mind. They are the result of attempts to find new flaws that have never before been imagined. Like all forms of knowledge, they become more complex over time: even though simple attacks still exist (SQL code injection remains the most common type of attack, due to how easy it is to execute), much more sophisticated scenarios have also begun to emerge. A single person or even a company will find it highly difficult to even just stay informed of all possible types of attack and prepare appropriate counter-measures, let alone anticipate these attacks independently.

It is probably simpler, less expensive and safer to rely on existing benchmarks.

Many commercial companies have chosen to specialize in vulnerability testing. In government contexts, Computer Emergency Response Teams (CERTs) [WIK 16a] have been founded and regularly publish notices detailing the security issues that they find. In France, the primary CERT is operated by ANSSI, but there are also other dedicated CERTs, e.g. one for the French academic research network.

CERTs inform us of vulnerabilities as they are discovered, but only rarely provide a comprehensive overview of the security measures that need to be taken.

There also exist archives of specifications designed to assist developers in their work. ANSSI published a document listing recommendations for securing websites [ANS 13]. Although this contains a wealth of information relating to general organization and log management, the recommendations remain fairly general, and their programming-related aspects are unspecific.

2.5.1. *ASVS requirements*

Fortunately, a non-profit American foundation, the Open Web Application Security Project (OWASP [OWA 15a]), has been working to make the web more secure, and offers a wide selection of tools and documents in open formats. This is probably the most comprehensive open-source reference for web application security.

Founded in 2001, it has been actively sponsored by major companies, including big names such as Adobe, Hewlett Packard, Saleforce and Oracle, but also by universities from all over the world.

Among other activities, the project regularly publishes a list of the top 10 most frequent types of web attack [OWA 13]. They also offer a tool for simulating attacks to test the robustness of an application or website.

Finally, the Application Security Verification Standard (ASVS) subproject has developed a grid of good practices that can be applied to web development projects [OWA 14a]. A summary of this was prepared by a contributor in the ODS format (the LibreOffice spreadsheet file type), with French translations available on the Internet [OWA 14b]. A French adaptation of version 3 is also available [QUI 16].

The security requirements listed in this document are categorized into three levels, depending on the complexity of their implementation or that of the attacks they are designed to foil.

Level 1, the *opportunistic* level, includes 82 items. These should be implemented in every web development project. They protect against so-called opportunistic attacks, i.e. attacks that are conducted randomly in order to find incidental security flaws.

Level 2, the *standard* level, lists 144 requirements, and is useful for applications that require a much higher security level. These measures protect against targeted attacks with relatively limited resources.

Level 3, *advanced*, presents 175 requirements that must necessarily be implemented in all critical projects. The objective of these measures is to achieve good robustness against complex attacks, and to set up mechanisms that are likely to identify and report suspicious behavior that might indicate attempted intrusion (sometimes referred to as weak signals).

Even meeting the opportunistic-level standards requires some thought and modifications to the code compared to a naive approach with no special protective measures. Level 2 is more difficult to achieve, and can require relatively complex procedures to be implemented, such as resource controllers that check whether operations are being processed within certain time parameters.

Level 3 on the other hand requires strong expertise, adequate resources and proven code architecture: this is far beyond what is achievable by web development performed "on the back of a napkin". Mobilizing development teams that specialize in security is essential for this.

2.5.2. *Determining the relevant causes and their likelihoods of occurrence*

Using the ASVS grid to determine the requirements that need to be considered during development cirumvents the need to determine the causes and likelihood of occurrence of an attack.

If there are no special stakes associated with an application, attackers will likely not be willing to devote significant lengths of time trying to penetrate it (unless they want to gain control of the company information system in search of more valuable data – but that is another story). Usually, they will not seek to orchestrate complex attack scenarios: the cost necessary to complete these scenarios would not be justified by the value of the data obtained or the damage caused.

However, a sensitive program might be targeted by sophisticated attacks whose development can afford higher time investment and resources.

The fact that the ASVS grid is divided into three levels therefore allows us to adjust the effort that we invest in securing an application as a function of the potential risk. The specific requirements listed under level 3 are designed to counter complex attack scenarios, but are also more complicated to implement than those listed under level 1.

In EBIOS terminology, by using this table, we are transferring the responsibility for estimating causes and occurrences to it, depending on the desired security level of our application.

2.5.3. *Choosing the level of requirements*

In the previous sections, we estimated the security needs and the impact of failure. It is tempting to use this information to define the level of security requirements.

Table 2.6 provides an example that allows us to quickly identify the category of an application.

Level	Description
High	The maximum impact in the event of a security failure is equal to 4
Standard	The maximum impact in the event of a security failure is equal to 3
Minimal or opportunistic	Other cases

Table 2.6. *Classification levels of the application*

Our security study has allowed us to determine the requirements that should be taken into consideration, which will strongly influence our approach to designing the application and launching it into production.

2.6. How should this study be performed in a company setting?

Applications are only one block within the larger information system: it is not possible to guarantee that an application is secure without considering the technical environment that hosts it: servers, networks, workstations if applicable, etc. However, the way that it is designed and the risks that it protects against can directly affect the reputation of the company, as well as company profits, etc.

The required security level cannot be defined by IT professionals on their own: the party requesting the application, who understands the need for it, is best placed to estimate the consequences of a security failure. Often, this step is performed by an approval procedure that is defined company-wide, at least in larger companies. We will not study this approval procedure in full detail here, as it is beyond the scope of this book. However, even without a formal procedure, it is always important for the software requester to be involved in defining the target security level.

In general, it is also important to conduct risk assessment at an early stage of the decision process that will ultimately lead to the realization of the application.

Risk assessment is an essential step: depending on its conclusions, changes in the software programming approach or the implementation of the host platform may be required.

This step must be performed by the functional project manager (also known as the project owner), and should be validated by the CEO or his/her representative: if a software program introduces high risks for the company, the decision to implement it should be taken by the highest authorities within the company. IT professionals can assist with this, but should not ever make the decision in place of the users or executives responsible for the program.

In French government administration, all information systems (including applications) must be approved for information system security before they are commissioned. This approval is issued by a competent entity responsible for information system security (referred to by the French acronym AQSSI), which is usually the director of the relevant structure. This approval certifies that the necessary measures have been taken to protect against the risks created by the application.

3

Encryption and Web Server Configuration

3.1. Examples of different web servers

The nature of web software programs, which send pages to the user's browser (also known as web servers), has changed dramatically in recent years.

The 2000s were dominated by competition between Apache software [APA 16] and Microsoft-based servers, Internet Information Server (IIS) [MIC 16].

Although Apache servers are now the most commonly used type of server, a newcomer, NGINX [NGI 16], has recently begun to gain in popularity, renowned for its performance. IIS has largely disappeared and is seldom used, except for very specific platforms.

Each of these servers is configured using different principles. Whereas Apache governs the behavior either from a global configuration file or from *.htaccess* files placed directly within the file system, NgInx works differently, with one single file for each application (website name), usually saved in the */etc/nginx/sites-enabled* folder. This makes code review easier: you do not need to browse the entire tree to determine the system configuration, but it also has disadvantages, especially in the context of hosting platforms. Specifying the desired settings is not always possible, since access to the file might be prohibited.

Each of these web servers can adopt the same configuration, even though the actual commands for doing so can differ. There would be little interest in giving one presentation for each type of server; we will only give examples for Apache, which is the most common, used by almost 50% of all active websites [NET 16].

3.2. Introduction to concepts in encryption

Encryption is the process of modifying a message so that it becomes incomprehensible to anybody who does not know the key or decryption method. We distinguish two main types of encryption: symmetric encryption, and its variant, hashing, and asymmetric encryption. The implementation of the latter is based on digital certificates.

3.2.1. *Symmetric encryption*

Symmetric encryption (or private-key encryption) uses the same key both to encrypt and decrypt the message.

A cipher is applied to the information being encrypted. One of the parameters of this cypher is a key known only by the sender and receiver (Figure 3.1).

Given the key and the cipher, the encrypted message can be decrypted by applying the inverse cipher associated with the key.

There are two techniques for doing this. Block ciphers divide the message into several parts of equal size (between 64 and 256 bits, depending on the algorithm). This is the most common type of encryption in computer systems. Stream ciphers encrypt the message bit by bit: this technique is mainly used for radio transmission systems (GSM – cellphone networks, Bluetooth – wireless networks, for example).

The size of the key itself is typically between 56 and 256 bits.

The strength of a symmetric cipher depends on several factors. The longer the key, the more secure the encryption. It is widely believed that a key of 256 bits (2^{256} is approximately 10^{77}, which is estimated to be close to the number of electrons in the universe) can never be broken by brute force, i.e. by testing each combination in turn. However, the length of the key is not the only factor that determines the strength of the cipher. Messages are encrypted block by block, and the larger each block, the more robust the cipher. The same computation function is also applied multiple times (number of iterations). The greater the number of iterations, the more robust the cipher; ANSSI recommends performing 65,000 iterations. The relevancy of the algorithm itself must also be considered, and the key must be generated completely at random.

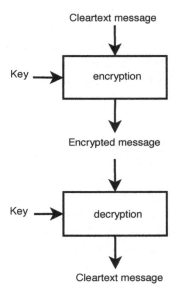

Figure 3.1. *Principle of symmetric encryption*

To improve security, especially for codes or passwords, limiting the number of permitted attempts is also a good idea. For example, smart cards are blocked after three unsuccessful attempts, which means that unlock codes with only 4–6 digits are sufficient.

Today, the most widely used algorithm is *AES256*: the blocks are 128 bits in size, and the key is 256 bits. It is currently believed to be secure.

Symmetric encryption is inexpensive in terms of computation time, due to the simplicity of its algorithms (matrix permutations and boolean XOR-type functions are applied to the data). However, they have a disadvantage: the sender and the receiver must first exchange the secret key. Over an Internet connection, confirming the identities of the sender and the receiver is problematic, and the key must be transmitted in such a way that nobody else can see it. We will see below that asymmetric encryption provides a solution to this problem.

3.2.2. *Computing hashes and salting passwords*

In computing, a hash is a fixed-length sequence of characters calculated from a file or an arbitrary sequence of characters. The hash is unique: it is impossible to obtain the same hash from different data. But if the algorithm is not sufficiently secure or the number of possible combinations is too small, there can be collisions, i.e. two different strings can lead to the same hash[1]. Finally, it should not be possible to reconstruct the original information from the hash.

There are two main situations in which hashes are useful. The first is when we wish to verify that a copy of a file is identical to the original, for example when downloading an ISO image. The website hosting the download indicates the hash value, and specifies the method used to calculate it. Once the file has been downloaded, it is easy to recalculate the hash and check that both values are identical. If there is a difference, the downloaded file is not identical to the original, either due to an error during transmission or interference from a hacker, which typically takes the form of a *man-in-the-middle* attack [WIK 15a]. In this type of attack, the attackers position themselves between the client's computer and the web server, and rewrite the transmitted information in real time.

Hashes are also used to encode passwords in such a way that they cannot be decoded.

A special procedure can be used to store passwords. When the password is created, its hash is calculated, and the hash is stored in the database. To check the password, the program calculates the hash of the string entered by the user, and then compares it to the value stored in the database. If the two hashes are identical, the password is accepted as correct (Figure 3.2).

---

1 Today, the *md5* algorithm is no longer used alone, primarily because of this weakness.

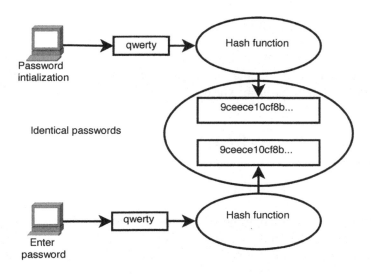

Figure 3.2. *Password verification using hashes*

Today, we extend this procedure with a technique known as salting. The hash is calculated from the data given to the hash algorithm. But if these data are predictable (password too easy to guess, for example), it can be relatively easy to recover the original data from the hash.

This can happen in practice for passwords. Too many people choose passwords that are easy to guess: the strings *password* or *12345678*, first names or the date of birth of a child or spouse, etc., are unfortunately very common choices. If an attacker knows the hashing algorithm and has access to the database following an intrusion or data theft, they will be able to run a search that will easily find some of these passwords.

To protect against the risk of this type of attack, one solution is to mix in a piece of variable information when the hash is calculated. This variable information is different for each user. This is called salting. Usually, the account or login id, which is necessarily unique, is appended to the password: even if two users have the same password, this procedure results in different hashes. Below is an example with the password *password* and the two distinct user accounts *john* and *mark* (the code was generated using a Linux command):

```
echo johnpassword|sha256sum
88071bcc...
```

We joined the username (*john*) and the password (*password*) together before computing the hash. We now do the same with a different username, *mark*:

```
echo markpassword|sha256sum
bd6e27fb08...
```

The two hashes are different.

Therefore, even though the passwords themselves might be the same, the values stored in the database are never identical. Even if the attacker knows the salting algorithm, they will be forced to recalculate all possible values for each account, which makes their task much more complex.

3.2.3. *Asymmetric encryption*

Symmetric encryption is secure enough to protect communications, but it suffers from a fundamental flaw: the encryption key must be shared between both parties. Thus, we need a way to exchange the key without it being intercepted, while verifying the identity of the person with whom we are communicating.

Asymmetric encryption provides a solution to this problem.

Asymmetric protocols generate two keys instead of one, based on two randomly chosen prime numbers. The remarkable property of this procedure is that a message encrypted with one key can only be decrypted using the other:

Alice   Bob

Figure 3.3. *Principle of asymmetric encryption*

The message encrypted with key 1 can only be decrypted with key 2. The reverse is also true: the message encrypted with key 2 can only be decrypted with key 1.

In practice, the first key is kept secret by its owner: it is referred to as the *private key*. The second key, the *public key*, is transmitted to all recipients that request it.

This mechanism provides an easy way of accomplishing two different tasks: encrypting messages and verifying the identity of a communication partner.

If Bob wants to send an encrypted message to Alice, he retrieves her public key, and uses it to encrypt his message. Alice can then decrypt the message using her private key: she is the only one able to do so, as she is the only one who knows the private key.

Now, if Alice sends a message to Bob, and Bob wants to be certain that it was definitely Alice who sent it, the procedure is a little more complicated (Figure 3.4).

The following sequence of operations is performed:

– Alice calculates the hash of her message using a hash function as discussed above;

– she encrypts the hash using her private key;

– she sends a message with the encrypted hash to Bob;

– Bob receives this message, and calculates its hash;

– he decrypts the encrypted hash sent by Alice using her public key;

– finally, he compares both hashes: if they are identical, then it must have been Alice who sent the message.

Of course, this protocol is carried out automatically, and these calculations are performed by software programs, such as email clients like Thunderbird [MOZ 15].

Asymmetric encryption is relatively robust because it is currently not possible to quickly factor the product of two prime numbers if they are chosen to be sufficiently large (there are other algorithms for managing asymmetric keys based on elliptic curves rather than prime numbers; these algorithms do not require the keys to be so large).

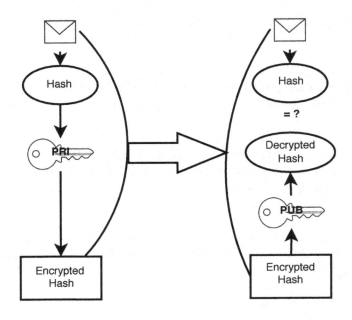

Figure 3.4. *Principle of asymmetric encryption-based signatures*

As it currently stands, the prime numbers used to generate the keys must have sizes of at least 2048 bits to guarantee that they are robust. Even today, ANSSI recommends using keys with 3096 bits, especially if they are intended to remain in usage until after 2030.

3.2.4. *What is the ideal length for encryption keys?*

The figures listed here are taken from a document published by ANSII [ANS 14].

Here are some examples that give an idea of the orders of magnitude involved.

2^n	10^n	Order of magnitude
2^{32}	4,294,967,296	Number of people on Earth
2^{46}	$7.036874418 \times 10^{13}$	Sun–Earth distance, in millimeters
2^{55}	$3.602879702 \times 10^{16}$	Number of operations performed in 1 year at a rate of one billion per second (1 Ghz)
2^{90}	$1.237940039 \times 10^{27}$	Number of operations performed in 15 billion years at a rate of one billion per second
2^{256}	$1.157920892 \times 10^{77}$	Estimated number of electrons in the universe

Table 3.1. *Some examples of orders of magnitude*

For secret-key encryption (symmetric keys), the minimum block size must be at least 64 bits (128 bits after 2020). The length of the encryption key must be at least 128 bits. It is believed that a key of length 256 bits will never be able to be broken by brute force.

The decryption rules for asymmetric encryption are completely different: factoring procedures are used, which are easier to compute. The minimum size of the prime moduli, i.e. the moduli used to generate the keys, should not be less than 2048 bits (3072 bits for certificates intended to remain in usage after 2030).

3.2.5. *Digital certificates and the chain of certification*

One of the problems with using asymmetric encryption lies in the fact that it is difficult to be sure that the public key, provided by Alice, is indeed hers and was not replaced by an attacker.

One solution is to trust a certification authority that guarantees the validity of the public key.

The certification authority signs Alice's public key using the following procedure:

– when Alice generates her two keys, she sends her public key to the certification authority;

– the certification authority verifies Alice's identity, for example by checking her identification documents, and then signs Alice's public key by encrypting its hash with the certification authority's own private key. The public key and the encrypted hash are stored in a *digital certificate*.

To verify that the digital certificate (and hence the public key) indeed belongs to Alice, her communication partner can calculate the hash of Alice's public key and then decrypt the encrypted hash using the public key of the certification authority. If these two hashes are identical, the user can trust that this key belongs to Alice, so long as they trust the certification authority. This is exactly the same procedure as for signing messages, as discussed just above (see section 3.2.3).

The public keys of the certification authorities are built directly into computer systems, which means they can be trusted without necessarily knowing all of them. Software publishers such as the Mozilla foundation for the Firefox browser are responsible for including integrated certificates issued by certification authorities. These public keys are technically implemented by placing them in a self-signed certificate, i.e. a certificate signed directly by the certification authority that created the key.

In most cases, the certification authorities do not use their private key to generate the certificates of their clients, but instead create an intermediate key that is then used to produce the required certificates. This leads to a chain of certification (Figure 3.5).

In this example, the server certificate is generated from a level 3 certificate. To allow the browser to validate the certificate submitted by the server, the server produces three certificates on request, which makes it possible to unravel the chain up to a known certification authority (the root certificate).

Certificates allow persons or devices to be reliably identified. They can therefore be used to authenticate users in applications, sign messages or documents and encrypt messages or communications to prevent them from being read by unauthorized parties. This is the procedure used for web applications, in the form of the https protocol (see section 3.4).

3.3. Generating and managing encryption certificates

3.3.1. *The OpenSSL library*

OpenSSL is a library of tools for managing TLS encryption. Distributed under the Apache license, it is available for almost every operating system, and is the most frequently used library in practical contexts.

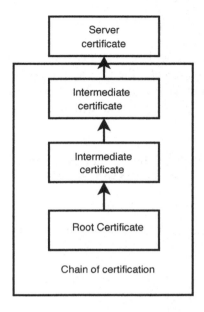

Figure 3.5. *The chain of certification*

3.3.2. *Different types of certificates*

Public keys, private keys and certificates are provided in various formats. The most common are listed below:

– DER: Used to encode X509 certificates written in ASN.1. Standard filename extensions: .der, .cer, .crt, .cert;

– PEM: Privacy Enhanced Mail. This is base64-encoded DER with added ASCII headers. Standard filename extensions: .pem, .cer, .crt, .cert;

– PKCS#12: *Personal Information Exchange Syntax Standard*. This is a standard for storing private keys, public keys and certificates, usually in password-protected form. The data are stored as binary. Filename extension: .p12, .pfx (for Microsoft).

Personal certificates are stored in the .p12 format. They contain both the private key and the public key, and so should always be password-protected.

3.3.3. *Generating certificates*

A certificate is a public key that has been signed by a certification authority. To create a certificate, the best solution is to submit a request to a recognized authority, but we can also self-sign our certificates by creating our own authority. In this case, browsers will not recognize the certificate as secure.

In our discussion, we will begin by signing our own public keys. This is our only option if we do not have access to a certification authority.

3.3.3.1. *Creating the root certificate*

We begin by creating the private key of the authority corresponding to the root certificate.

```
openssl req -new -x509 -keyout cacert.pem -out
    cacert.pem -days 3650
```

This command generates a *private key - public key* pair. When this program is executed, it will request a password: this is the password used to protect the private key, which will need to be given each time that a certificate is signed. Here, the root certificate is valid for 10 years (3650 days).

The *cacert.pem* file contains both the private key and the public key.

We will now generate the certificate belonging to the certification authority, which will be used to validate the other certificates that we will generate subsequently; this certificate therefore contains the public key of the certification authority:

```
openssl x509 -in cacert.pem -out cacert.crt
```

The root certificate is the file *cacert.crt*.

3.3.3.2. *Creating the private and public keys of the server*

We will now generate the key pair (private key and public key), e.g. for a web server:

```
openssl genrsa  -out server.key 2048
```

The key has a length of 2048 bits.

We can protect it to prevent anyone other than *root* or authorized *processes* from accessing it:

```
chmod 600 server.key
```

The *private key - public key* pair does not have an expiration date, unlike certificates, which are issued for limited periods.

3.3.3.3. *Creating the request for a certificate to be validated by the root authority*

Using the key pair that we just generated, we will prepare a request to be submitted to the certification authority. It contains the public key, but also other information, including the name of the server or website for which we want to generate a key:

```
openssl req -new -key server.key -out server.csr
```

After running this command, we will need to fill out a few fields. To leave a field blank, we use a period (.).

```
Country Name (2 letter code) [AU]:US
State or Province Name (full name) [Some-State]:.
Locality Name (eg, city) []:.
Organization Name (eg, company) [Internet Widgits
    Pty Ltd]: MY COMPANY
Organizational Unit Name (eg, section) []: .
Common Name (eg, YOUR name) []:myserver.company.
    com
Email Address []: .

Please enter the following 'extra' attributes
to be sent with your certificate request
A challenge password []:
An optional company name []:
```

The last two fields are left blank. The *challenge password* is used to generate a password to unlock the private key, and is not required in this example.

Carefully note: it is important for the *Common Name* to match the name of the server or website that will be used. When verifying the key, the software will check that the server or website name is identical to the value stored in this field.

Some certification authorities allow multiple names to be specified here, which allows the same certificate to be used with multiple DNS entries. This is sometimes used for mail servers, enabling them to use the same certificate for both TLS pop access (*pop.myserver.com*) and webmail (*webmail.myserver.com*), etc. It is also possible to create certificates with *wildcard* characters, such as **.mydomain.com*: all subsites of this domain can be validated by the same certificate. Doing this is now officially discouraged because of the risks that it creates: if the certificate is hijacked, all of the websites of a single organization can now be forged.

Multiple certificates can also be created from the same *private key – public key* pair: one request is submitted for each web address hosted by the server.

3.3.3.4. *Signing the certificate locally*

If you do not wish to use the services of a registration authority, you need to generate the certificate yourself. The first time that you do this, you will need to create a file containing the serial numbers of the generated certificates (the *cacert.srl* file) as well as the certificates themselves, using the following command:

```
openssl x509 -req -in server.csr -CA cacert.pem -
    CAkey cacert.pem -out server.crt -
    Cacreateserial
```

If the *cacert.srl* file exists, the command for doing this is:

```
openssl x509 -req -days 3650 -in server.csr -CA
    cacert.pem -out server.crt
```

The *server.crt* file is a certificate that contains not just the public key itself, but also its hash, encrypted with the root certificate.

3.3.3.5. *Requesting a certificate signature from a registration authority*

If you have a certification authority, you can send them the file containing the certificate request (*server.csr*). In return, you will receive a certificate containing both the public key and its encrypted hash. Usually, the fields *Organization Name* and *Organizational Unit Name* are mandatory: check with your certification authority to know which fields are required.

You will also need to obtain the root certificate (the equivalent of *cacert.crt*, the public key of the certification authority), which will allow you to verify the validity of the certificate.

3.3.3.6. *Creating a self-signed certificate without using a registration authority*

Some applications need a simple self-signed certificate, i.e. one that is not signed by a registration authority, even a personal one. Once the certificate creation request has been executed, run the following command:

```
openssl x509 -req -days 3650 -in server.csr -
    signkey server.key -out server.crt
```

The file *server.crt* contains the self-signed certificate.

3.3.4. *Where are keys and certificates stored?*

In Linux-based systems using the *OpenSSL* library, the following folders are usually used:

– */etc/ssl/certs*: contains certificates and public keys. This folder is readable by all device users.

– */etc/ssl/private*: contains the private key(s) of the device.

Access to this second folder needs to be strictly managed: if somebody obtains the private key, they can decrypt all encrypted messages, or impersonate the sender. This type of attack is known as *man in the middle* [WIK 15a].

By default, this folder can only be accessed by the *root* account, which prevents web server processes from accessing the private keys, meaning that it will not be able to initiate *https* connections.

To change this behavior, we need to allow the *ssl-cert* group to browse this folder, and give private key read permissions to this group:

```
sudo chmod g+x ssl-cert /etc/ssl/private
sudo chmod g+r ssl-cert /etc/ssl/private/*
```

The *sudo* command grants administrative rights for executing commands.

Now, the account used by the web server, which in this case is *www-data*, is added to the *ssl-cert* group:

```
sudo usermod -a -G ssl-cert www-data
```

After restarting the Apache server, it will be able to access the private key and correctly manage *https* connections.

3.3.5. *Commands for viewing keys and certificates*

To view the contents of a private key:

```
openssl rsa -in server.key -text

Private-Key: (2048 bit)
modulus:
    00:bb:6c:c9:c5:57:4f:f3:7c:83:56:a9:2d:c1:5d:
(...)
publicExponent: 65537 (0x10001)
privateExponent:
    07:d3:12:d9:5a:3b:cc:3e:76:7d:37:b2:e1:4f:b2:
(...)
prime1:
    00:e4:40:84:cf:08:d9:b5:c8:2e:74:a3:3f:75:72:
(...)
exponent1:
    23:be:72:cd:d5:2d:fa:c8:a1:75:c4:86:d0:86:a1:
(...)
coefficient:
    58:c0:2b:ea:71:eb:a5:60:e0:a0:25:f5:7c:b1:94:
(...)
    75:53:08:da:ea:e1:74:6d
writing RSA key
-----BEGIN RSA PRIVATE KEY-----
```

```
MIIEogIBAAKCAQEAu2zJxVdP83yDVqktwVOsaR1QafKL+
    XblgtQT8pHDx2XQCWdW
(...)
IK/QeXnadKjz8jZT78nxL+N1xqK5RSBaAsk/
    hzQsdVMI2urhdGO=
-----END RSA PRIVATE KEY-----
```

To view the associated public key:

```
openssl rsa -in server.key -pubout
```

```
writing RSA key
-----BEGIN PUBLIC KEY-----
MIIBIjANBgkqhkiG9w0BAQEFAAOCAQ
(...)
OwIDAQAB
-----END PUBLIC KEY-----
```

To view a certificate:

```
openssl x509 -in server.crt -text -noout
```

```
Certificate:
    Data:
        Version: 1 (0x0)
        Serial Number: 16235780570068490813 (0
            xe15114685a1f1a3d)
    Signature Algorithm: sha256WithRSAEncryption
        Issuer: C=FR, CN=equinton
        Validity
            Not Before: Jun 22 15:35:19 2016 GMT
            Not After : Jun 20 15:35:19 2026 GMT
        Subject: C=FR, CN=equinton
        Subject Public Key Info:
            Public Key Algorithm: rsaEncryption
                Public-Key: (2048 bit)
                Modulus:
                    00:bb:6c:c9:c5:57:4f:f3:7c:83:
(...)
```

```
            Exponent: 65537 (0x10001)
   Signature Algorithm: sha256WithRSAEncryption
      23:29:ee:e1:6b:50:2c:d9:9e:6b:4c:10:2e
            :84:cc
(...)
```

To check the validity of the certificate:

```
openssl verify -CAfile cacert.crt server.crt
```

```
server.crt: OK
```

3.4. Implementing the HTTPS protocol

3.4.1. *Understanding the HTTPS protocol*

Today, digital communications require a certain minimum threshold of confidentiality (to protect passwords, bank details, etc.). The principle of the HTTPS protocol, which was originally *HTTP over SSL* and is now *HTTP over TLS* [WIK 15h] (SSL was abandoned as it is no longer considered to be secure), is to encrypt all communications.

TLS is a symmetric-key-based encryption procedure that meets this need perfectly. Its only shortcoming, like all symmetric-key protocols, is that the key must first be exchanged between both parties without being intercepted.

To achieve this, the designers proposed starting the dialogue by using asymmetric encryption. Figure 3.6 gives a slightly simplified diagram of the protocol.

Suppose a browser wishes to connect to a web server by HTTPS (usually the web server redirects the browser to the HTTPS protocol, but the result is the same). It retrieves the certificate provided by the web server and then checks its validity by decrypting the hash using the public key of the certification authority. If the certificate is not recognized, the browser displays a warning message and asks the user to confirm before accessing the requested page.

If the certificate is valid, the browser generates a symmetric key using the TLS protocol. It then encrypts it using the public key of the server and sends it to the server.

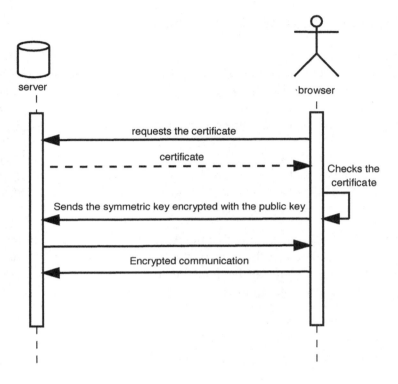

Figure 3.6. *Principle of the HTTPS protocol*

The server retrieves the key and then decrypts it using its private key: information can now be exchanged confidentially between the server and the browser.

In practice, the server sends other information along with the certificate, such as a list of accepted symmetric encryption protocols.

With this procedure, only the server has to justify its identity, and only the server has to present a digital certificate. However, some implementations of the HTTPS protocol require the client to also present a certificate. This is in particular used for direct communications between servers for automatically exchanging messages.

3.4.2. *Implementing the HTTPS protocol*

The HTTPS protocol relies on digital certificates. To protect an application, you must first obtain a certificate. This certificate contains the exact name of the application's web address, for example *my_application.com*. This allows the browser to check that the given certificate matches the name of the requested website.

The certificate must also be provided by a recognized certification authority: otherwise, the browser will indicate that it was not able to verify the certificate. This is because the chain of certification, as presented above (see section 3.2.5), is not complete.

The next step is to make sure that the Apache server redirects all requests sent by the *http* protocol to the *https* protocol. This is done in the virtual host configuration file, which can be found in the */etc/apache2/sites-available* folder. Here is an example configuration:

```
<VirtualHost *:80>
    ServerName myapp.com
    ServerPath /myapp.com
    RewriteEngine On
    RewriteRule ^ https://myapp.com/%{REQUEST_URI}
        [R]
</VirtualHost>
```

Now, all content sent via HTTP, i.e. to port 80, is instead redirected to the HTTPS protocol. To do this, we use the URL rewrite function (*Rewrite*).

We will now see how to configure the access to our application in HTTPS mode:

```
<VirtualHost *:443>
    ServerName myapp.com
    ServerPath /myapp.com
    ServerAdmin admin@myapp.com
    ServerSignature off
```

The *VirtualHost* command now points to port 443, which is reserved for HTTPS. We also see a few general-purpose commands, one of which shows the name of the site administrator (a generic address).

The *ServerSignature off* command hides the version of the Apache server.

Support for the HTTPS protocol is enabled using the commands:

```
SSLEngine on
SSLCertificateFile /etc/ssl/certs/myapp.cert
SSLCertificateKeyFile /etc/ssl/private/myapp.
   key
SSLCACertificateFile /etc/ssl/certs/cachain.
   pem
```

We can also see the certificate access paths: *SSLCertificateFile* is the certificate (signed public key), *SSLCertificateKeyFile* is the private key and *SSLCACertificateFile* is the file containing the chain of certification, i.e. the public keys of each authority that signed the public key.

Now, we must specify where the application code is located, using the following command:

```
DocumentRoot /var/www/myappApp/myapp
```

And finally, application-specific log files:

```
CustomLog /var/log/apache2/myapp-access.log
   combined
ErrorLog /var/log/apache2/myapp-error.log
</VirtualHost>
```

All access information is stored in the file */var/log/apache2/myapp-access.log*, (*combined* specifies the choice of format for the log file), and the errors are logged in the file */var/log/apache2/myapp-error.log*.

3.4.3. *Testing the SSL chain*

Once the certificates have been successfully added and Apache has been configured, it is informative to check that the encryption has been correctly configured. Several tools are available to do this, either in downloadable form to test the configuration of an intranet, or directly online. With the latter, we simply need to give the address of the web server, then the website launches a more or less comprehensive analysis, first checking the chain of certification and then the protocols being used. SSLLABS [LAB 16] offers possibly one of the most comprehensive tools. This allows us to identify any obsolete protocols that might still be accepted by the server and yields a list of compatible operating systems and browsers.

3.5. Improving the security of the Apache server

In this section, we will briefly discuss how to improve the security of the Apache web server. This is not an exhaustive guide to system administration, but simply gathers together a few useful principles: system administrators are likely to be aware of all of these things, but might nonetheless appreciate a checklist to ensure that nothing has been forgotten.

The configurations listed below are for a Linux server running Ubuntu Server 14.04 LTS.

3.5.1. *Ensuring that the server hosting Apache has the latest security updates*

When a server is first installed, it is usually up-to-date with the latest security patches. However, since new vulnerabilities are continuously being discovered, servers need to be updated regularly, generally at least once a day. For Ubuntu or Debian-type distributions, we can use the *unattended-upgrades* package, which was specifically designed to automate this process.

This package uses the */etc/apt/apt.conf.d /50unattended-upgrades* file to specify all of the parameters used to configure the update software. This can be used to specify the following, among other things:

– which repositories should be used to perform updates. Typically, for a server, we should only install security updates;

– whether there are any packages that should not be updated: this is often the case for the *libc* library, which is essential for the system to operate properly; any changes to this component can cause significant disruption;

– whether the device should restart after an update that requires it (usually after installing a new kernel). If this is enabled, it is possible to specify the time at which the server should restart. Automatically restarting protects against vulnerabilities in the kernels themselves, which can result in denial of service or privilege escalation attacks. However, restarting is a complex operation, especially in virtual environments where servers share resources, and it is advisable to ensure beforehand that the operation can be completed safely.

There are also other settings, for example for sending emails, which we will not discuss here.

3.5.2. *Prohibiting low-security protocols*

In the 1990s, the American government banned the export of strong security protocols outside of its territory. This led people to use less secure protocols. At the time, this was not a problem, but, with the computing power available today, they have become easy to circumvent.

To remain compatible with existing websites, the Apache web server continues to allow all types of protocol. Unfortunately, even if secure certificates are used, Apache will continue to use weakly encrypted connections, unless these connections are disallowed.

To do this, we must edit the configuration file */etc/apache2/sites-available/ default-ssl* and add the following lines to the section beginning with *<VirtualHost _default_:443>*:

```
SSLProtocol All -SSLv2 -SSLv3
SSLHonorCipherOrder On
SSLCipherSuite ECDHE-RSA-AES128-SHA256:AES128-GCM-
    SHA256:HIGH:EECDH+AESGCM:EDH+AESGCM:AES256+
    EECDH:AES256+EDH:!MD5:!aNULL:!EDH:!RC4
SSLCompression off
```

The first line disables the SSL protocol, which is considered to be obsolete, and instead imposes TLS. The next two lines force the use of the SHA256 signing algorithm (the default is SHA-1, which uses 128-bit keys), as well as other new protocols that are considered to be reliable. Finally, the last command disables SSL compression, which can create security issues (this directive is usually set to *off* by default).

Remy van Elst discusses these questions further in a fairly comprehensive article on comprehensively securing SSL connections with Apache2 [ELS 15].

Today, there are websites that generate configurations adapted to the usage context (web server, supported browsers, etc.). For example, the one provided by the Mozilla foundation [MOZ 16b] is particularly comprehensive. Referring to these tools makes it easier to stay ahead of advancements in encryption technologies.

3.5.3. *Preventing request flooding*

One of the simplest ways of "taking down" a server, i.e. preventing it from responding to queries, is to send a burst of tens of thousands of requests simultaneously. This is called a denial-of-service attack.

The Apache *evasive* module counters these types of attack. It blocks identical requests sent within a give unit of time, and limits the number of requests from the same user, again per unit time.

This module is easy to install:

```
sudo apt-get install libapache2-mod-evasive
```

Its parameters can be configured in the file */etc/apache2/mods-available/evasive.conf.*

Here are example values (the default values are shown in brackets):

– *DOSHashTableSize* (3097): size of the table used to record calls;

– *DOSPageCount* (2): number of requests called in a given unit of time by the same user. The default value is usually sufficient unless the same component is called multiple times from within a single page;

– *DOSSiteCount* (50): number of calls to the website within a given unit of time, summed over all pages;

– *DOSPageInterval* (1): time interval, in seconds, used to count the number of requests;

– *DOSSiteInterval* (1): time interval used to count all incoming requests;

– *DOSBlockingPeriod* (10): period, in seconds, which blocked users will not be able to complete requests.

To make the module work, each of the parameters must be activated by uncommenting them before restarting the Apache server.

With the default parameter values, if a user sends two identical requests to the server within 1 s, they will be blocked for 10 s. They will also be blocked if they send more than 50 requests per second.

Whenever a request is blocked, a message is saved in the error log file */var/log/apache2/error.log*:

```
[Thu Jun 23 09:21:08.539066 2016] [evasive20:error
] [pid 19145] [client ::1:54188] client denied
by server configuration: /var/www/html/eabxcol/
display/images/logo.png, referer: https://
localhost/eabxcol/index.php?module=management
```

The *referer* specifies the page that was originally called, i.e. the one that was blocked.

The advantage of this module is that the server will use very few resources if the threshold is exceeded: the request will not be completed, and the processing time will be very short.

It is usually installed in the *reverse-proxy* server, which acts as a gateway for all applications or websites associated with the organization. Since it is still executed on the server itself, it is only effective up to a certain point: if the attack is truly massive, the server resources will eventually be overwhelmed anyway. Other, more complex techniques can be implemented, but require modifications to the actual network equipment, or even at the level of the Internet Service Provider (ISP).

Like any protective measure, one should first consider whether the risk justifies implementing other measures in addition to this module.

3.5.4. *Implementing a request filter*

Apache proposes a module, *mod_security*, for analyzing the requests received by the server and filtering them, if required, before forwarding them to the PHP engine. This is called the application firewall, which acts as an interface before the actual connection to the web server.

This module can be complex to configure, but examples of basic configurations are available.

First, it needs to be installed on the server:

```
sudo apt-get install libapache2-mod-security2
```

The Apache server automatically restarts, but the module is not yet operational: no directives have been defined. The default root configuration file is located in the */etc/modsecurity* folder, and needs to be renamed to be visible to the module:

```
cd /etc/modisecurity
sudo cp modsecurity.conf-recommended modsecurity.
   conf
```

You will need to modify the contents of this file to suit your own configuration. To allow files of up to 64 MB to be downloaded, you need to modify the following directive:

```
SecRequestBodyLimit 67108864
```

We will now activate the basic directives used by the module. Type the following commands:

```
for f in 'ls /usr/share/modsecurity-crs/base_rules
   /*' ; do sudo ln -s $f ; done
```

and restart the Apache server:

```
sudo service apache2 restart
```

By default, the module is configured to only register abnormal events (directive *SecRuleEngine DetectionOnly* in the file *modsecurity.conf*). You can test that the program properly detects anomalies, for example by entering the string; *or 1 = 1-* - into a submitted field (this command represents an SQL injection attack (see section 4.2.1)). An entry will be created in the log file */etc/apache2/modsec_audit.log*.

Check the log file, and disable any modules that you do not wish to use by removing their links.

Very well-written English documentation is available from DigitalOcean [DIG 15]. You can also visit the official project website [MOD 15].

You should test this module before activating it on a production server. Check the log files that it generates in particular (they can become large very quickly), and only activate the modules that you actually need.

If your application is properly coded and secured, and basic precautions have been taken directly in Apache, this module may not necessarily be useful to you. However, for open-source applications taken from the net, it can be invaluable. For example, room booking software written several years ago might not necessarily include the latest protections against the most common types of attack, such as SQL injection. Rather than rewriting it or investing time in modifying its code to make it secure, it is likely more beneficial to set it up behind an application firewall such as *modsecurity*. If this firewall is properly configured, it will block most common types of attack.

Of course, this approach should only be used for low-priority applications that pose limited risk in the event that an attack should succeed.

3.5.5. *Allowing page header modifications*

Modern browsers are now capable of implementing several different security checks, provided that the server asks for them to be activated. They are disabled by default because, in some cases, they can prevent applications from working.

The checks are, for example, designed to limit the risk that cookies from other webpages are stolen using specially designed scripts written in

JavaScript. To ask the browser to implement these precautions, they need to be included in the HTML header sent by the web server.

To allow the application to modify HTML headers, we first need to load a module to complement Apache, using the following commands:

```
a2enmod headers
service apache2 restart
```

Below, we will see which instructions should be used to improve the protection of the application.

3.5.6. Authorizing .htaccess files

.htaccess files allow us to modify the behavior of the Apache server in individual folders. This is mainly used to prevent access to critical folders, e.g. the folder that contains the connection details for the database.

Since these files contain special instructions, we must ask Apache to allow them to be executed.

Usually, when a new application is installed on a server, a new virtual site is registered in the */etc/apache2/sites-available* folder using a configuration file. This file indicates, among other things, the physical location of the application within the server and specifies various parameters, such as encryption certificates for *https* connections. We need to make sure that this file contains the following instructions:

```
<Directory /myfolder>
        AllowOverride all
        Order allow,deny
        allow from all
</Directory>
```

The first instruction, *AllowOverride*, allows all Apache directives in the folder */myfolder* to be overridden, which ensures that all of the *.htaccess* files of the application are correctly taken into account.

3.5.7. *Hiding the version information of Apache and PHP*

Allowing attackers to view the versions of installed software gives them valuable information, especially if everything is not fully up-to-date. If we are using an obsolete version of PHP that is known to be vulnerable to a particular type of attack, revealing the version number tells the attackers exactly how to penetrate the system.

It is easy to check whether a web application is displaying its version numbers by installing the *wappAlyzer* [WAP 15] module in the Firefox browser. This module collects information about all components of the application and the server: the operating system, web engine, language and all third-party software components, such as *JQuery* [JQU 15]. If the version numbers are not hidden, this module will show them.

To prevent the Apache server and its PHP module from revealing their version numbers, we simply need to edit the configuration files. For Apache, we need to edit the file */etc/apache2/conf.d/security*, and check the configuration of the following parameters:

```
ServerTokens Prod
ServerSignature Off
```

PHP can be configured by modifying the following parameter in the */etc/php5/apache2/php.ini* file:

```
expose_php = Off
```

Apache must then be restarted for these changes to take effect.

3.6. In summary

Applications can never be considered to be intrinsically safe: their run-time environment plays a significant role in their overall security.

Nowadays, encryption is essential for protecting applications. Only allowing access in *https* mode is a necessary first step, but is not enough: the web server must also be properly configured to disallow obsolete protocols.

Setting up measures such as the Apache *evasive* mode or an application firewall strengthens the security of the application, provided that these measures are configured correctly. Launching an application into production requires close collaboration between the system administrators and developers. The needs of both parties must be taken into account. This will allow a good balance between performance and protection to be achieved.

4

Threats and Protecting Against Them

The most common threats to websites and web applications are known and documented. The OWASP project regularly publishes a list of the top 10 most frequent attacks. Their last list was published in 2013 [OWA 13].

Many attacks directly target the application code, such as injection-based attacks, which have held first place in the list for years now, whereas others focus on the web server configuration. Poorly encrypted or unencrypted connections make things much easier for attackers; they just have to intercept the packets circulating on the network to obtain the information they want.

Naturally, encryption is the first measure that should be implemented server-side, but encryption should not be used to obscure other, more subtle mechanisms.

We will go over a few types of attack and ways of protecting against them without attempting to give an exhaustive discussion: the security field is constantly changing, and it would be presumptuous to claim to have thought of everything.

Although we will not discuss it here, managing the security of applications developed for smartphones requires special rules. OWASP has published guidelines for this kind of software. Indeed, one of the major risks associated with the proliferation of smartphone applications is that third-party applications can attempt to steal information from other applications. For example, an ordinary video game might try to extract information from a professional software application, which could then be used to mount an attack on a company.

4.1. The threats associated with web-based environments

We will not be able to give a detailed discussion of every threat that proper web server configuration can thwart, but we will consider some of them. Most directives are stored in the *.htaccess* file located in the application root folder, but they can also be placed in the configuration file, in the */etc/apache2/sites-available* folder.

4.1.1. *Limiting the types of authorized request*

The HTML protocol defines four main types of request:

– GET, for retrieving information;

– PUT, for sending new information;

– POST, for modifying existing information;

– DELETE, for deleting information.

All four of these request types are used by implementations of RESTful services (*Representational State Transfer*, which belong to the family of *web services*). These services are used to retrieve or modify information from other web applications without an input interface. For example, displaying a location or a map from *Google Maps* can be achieved with an application based on this technology.

However, traditional web applications only use GET and POST requests: to prevent attacks that use other types of request, the simplest approach is just to disable them. This can be done by adding a few lines to the *.htaccess* file:

```
<LimitExcept GET POST>
Deny from all
</LimitExcept>
```

This disables everything except GET and POST requests.

4.1.2. *Preventing users from browsing the website file system*

By default, web servers are configured to display the entire subdirectory tree of a folder if the request does not specify a page and the directory does not have a default file (such as *index.html* or *index.php*).

If this behavior is not disabled, attackers can explore the full website tree, and might find poorly protected files or useful information.

Therefore, it is highly recommended to add the following command:

```
Options  - Indexes
```

The minus symbol indicates that browsing the file system is forbidden.

4.1.3. *Limiting the risk of session cookie hijacking*

The HTML protocol is a *stateless* protocol, which means that each request sent to the server is processed independently. To track individual users, the server needs to implement a session mechanism.

When a session is created, a small file containing a unique identifier is sent to the browser. This is known as a cookie. It is systematically resubmitted to the server with each new request: this allows the program to associate the request with a specific execution environment.

Applications need this procedure in order to work properly. Without it, each time that the user needs to access a protected page, the password would need to be re-entered, since the server would be incapable of remembering logins.

But, unfortunately, if this cookie is stolen, the attacker will be able to impersonate the original user. The first countermeasure that should be taken to prevent this is to only send session cookies over the HTTPS protocol. Two parameters can be specified to PHP to enforce this, by adding the *php_flag* command to the *.htaccess* file:

```
php_flag  session . cookie_httponly  on
php_flag  session . cookie_secure  on
```

The first command indicates that the cookie should only be transmitted over HTTP, and the second specifies that it should only be sent to the browser if the HTTP protocol is encrypted (HTTPS mode).

We will see later that these instructions can also be coded directly in PHP when managing the session (see section 4.2.2).

4.1.4. *Hiding error messages*

Despite taking every care in the code, errors can happen. Even just a random database issue can cause an application to stop working.

Typically, an error message is generated automatically when an unexpected event occurs. If these error messages are displayed on the user's screen, attackers might obtain information that helps them to understand the inner workings of the program and its implementation. This is a risk worth avoiding.

The following PHP command can be added directly to the program code to stop error messages from being shown, but it can also be useful to add it to the *.htaccess* file:

```
php_flag display_errors Off
```

4.1.5. *Asking browsers to enable safeguards*

Browser publishers have developed increasingly sophisticated protective measures to keep their users safe. However, since these measures can stop certain applications from working, they are not always enabled by default. The application must ask the browser to enable them.

This is done by sending special instructions to the browser encoded into the HTTP header of the message.

Rewriting these headers with Apache requires the *Headers* module, which we configured earlier (see section 3.5.5). The first set of instructions protects the local cache, either by disabling caching, or by preventing the cache from being accessed by third parties.

```
Header set Cache-Control "max-age=0, no-cache, no-
    store, must-revalidate, private"
Header set Pragma "no-cache"
<FilesMatch "\.(ico|pdf|flv|jpg|jpeg|png|gif|js|
    css|swf)$">
    Header set Cache-Control "max-age=604800,
        private"
</FilesMatch>
```

The first two instructions disable caching in all cases: each new page and download must be resent to the browser each time. The difference between the instructions lies in the protocols that they support: *Pragma* was used by version 1.0 of the *http* protocol, and *cache-control* is implemented for versions 1.1 and higher.

It can be beneficial to store files containing images, stylesheets, etc., which are shared by the majority of the application pages in the browser cache: this reduces the volume of the data that needs to be exchanged between the server and the computer. The *FileMatch* section analyzes file extensions (using a regular expression), and authorizes caching if the transmitted file matches one of the specified extensions. In our case, the cache is configured to have a maximum age of 7 days (in seconds), but is set to private, which means that it can only be accessed by the application (address) that created it.

Some attacks attempt to load invisible frames onto the screen and place them between a legitimate webpage and the user. When the user clicks on a button or enters a password, the information is intercepted by the malicious frame. To avoid this behavior, it is a good idea to ask the browser to ensure that frames and the content they display have the same origin as the original page. This can be done with the following command:

```
Header set X-Frame-Options SAMEORIGIN
```

The following two commands are specific to Microsoft and Internet Explorer:

```
Header set X-XSS-Protection: "1; mode=block"
Header set X-Content-Type-Options: "nosniff"
```

The first limits the risk of XSS attacks, which we will discuss later (see section 4.2.3). This attack involves injecting malicious code into a page to redirect the user to the attacker's website.

The second command disables the default behavior of Internet Explorer, which redefines the MIME type of documents, ignoring any instructions that are given to it. The MIME type is a convention for identifying the type of transmitted documents: text files, images, programs and so on. MIME types are standardized.

Usually, the MIME type is sent by the server to the browser together with files, which tells the browser what it needs to do with the files. Unlike other browsers, Internet Explorer analyzes the file and attempts to automatically select the most appropriate MIME type. Thus, text files risk being misinterpreted as web pages, as do maliciously constructed images. If the text file or image contains instructions that might be executed by the HTML interpreter, the attack is highly likely to succeed. This is typically used for XSS attacks. The *nosniff* option asks Internet Explorer to stop analyzing MIME types and instead use those specified by the server.

4.2. The top 10 most frequent attacks in 2013

We will now examine each of the most common types of attack in detail, and see how we can protect ourselves against them. This list is based on the list published by OWASP in 2013 [OWA 13]. It is not exhaustive, but is sufficiently broad to cover most of the risks that we are likely to encounter today. We will present the attacks in order of decreasing frequency.

Once again, there is no miracle solution that provides perfect protection. We will introduce some precautions in the implementation and the configuration files, others in the code structure, and yet others by observing good coding practices. We have already mentioned some of these protective measures, in particular those that relate to the web server configuration.

4.2.1. *Code injection*

This attack deliberately modifies the values sent to the server in such a way as to influence the way that they are processed. This can reveal information that was not intended to be visible by the developer. The most common type of attack is SQL code injection, which we will describe in detail, but code injection is also possible with XML files, or queries to LDAP directories, a popular standard for managing company directories.

This is the most common type of attack because it is the easiest to implement, and applications can very easily be left vulnerable to it; simply forgetting to implement a check can be enough to create an opening for attacks. If successful, injection attacks can reveal a large quantity of information or allow a user's password to be guessed.

We will consider a few examples to demonstrate how a simple attack might unfold. The following SQL command can be used to verify the login and password of an account:

```
$name = 'smith';
$password = "qwerty";
SELECT id FROM accounts WHERE name = '$name' AND
    password = '$password';
```

Normally, when the variables *$name* (value *smith*) and *$password* (value *qwerty*) are evaluated, this becomes:

```
SELECT id FROM accounts WHERE name = 'smith' AND
    password = 'qwerty';
```

Of course, in practice, nobody should use *qwerty* as a password, and the password should be hashed (see section 3.2.2), as discussed above.

Now, suppose an attacker wishes to login using the account name *smith*, but does not know the password. He or she can change the string $name into **smith';–**. The query becomes:

```
$name = "smith';--";
$password = 'unknown';
SELECT id FROM accounts WHERE name = 'smith';--'
    AND password = 'unknown';
```

Since the semicolon ends the statement, and the two dashes mark the rest of the line as a comment, the command actually executed by the server becomes:

```
SELECT id FROM accounts WHERE name = 'smith';
```

This circumvents the password check.

To protect against this simple example of code injection, we need to escape the apostrophe, i.e. replace it with a code sequence that will not be interpreted as an separator by the database server. Depending on the system, the apostrophe can be escaped by doubling it, or by preceding it with the \ character. If the apostrophe is escaped, the following code is sent to the server:

```
SELECT id FROM accounts WHERE name = 'smith\';--'
   AND password = 'unknown';
```

This query will return empty, since there are no users named *smith';–*.

PHP offers a range of functions for encoding quotes, some of which are specific to particular databases, and others that are general-purpose. The following script gives an example of how an array of variables can be handled:

```
function encodeData($connection, $data,
   $databaseType="pgsql") {
   if (is_array ( $data )) {
      /*
       *    Encode arrays
       */
      foreach ( $data as $key => $value ) {
         $data [$key] = $this->encodeData ( $value
            );
      }
   } else {
      /*
       * Encode strings
       */
         if ($this->typeDatabase == 'pgsql') {
            if (mb_detect_encoding ( $value ) != "
               UTF-8")
               $data = mb_convert_encoding ( $data
                  , 'UTF-8' );
```

```
        $data = pg_escape_string ( $connection ,
            $data );
      } else {
        $data = addslashes ( $data );
      }
   }
   return $data;
}
```

This is a recursive function: it can be applied to nested arrays. It is suitable for PostgreSQL databases, but *pg_escape_string* can be replaced by the function *mysqli_real_escape_string (mysqli $link , string $data)* so that it can be used with MySQL.

We saw our first example of injection above, using a string of characters. But it is just as easy to modify queries that take numbers as arguments.

Consider a second example:

```
$id = 1254;
$password = "qwerty";
UPDATE accounts SET password = '$password' WHERE
   id = $id;
```

This is an example of an update query, which might, for example, be used to change a password. Once the variables have been evaluated, the following query will be executed:

```
UPDATE accounts SET password = 'qwerty' WHERE id =
   1254;
```

This modifies the password of the account with id 1254.

But suppose we replace **1254** by the value **id**. The query then becomes:

```
UPDATE accounts SET password = 'qwerty' WHERE id =
   id;
```

Since the WHERE condition has become an equality (*id* is always equal to *id*), all of the passwords in the table will be changed.

One solution for protecting against this in the PHP code is to check that the index is greater than 0 (this holds for all automatically generated indices in modern SQL databases):

```
if ($id > 0) {
(...)
```

This test will work correctly if the *$id* variable doesn't begin with a number. However, if the value *1254 or 1 = 1;–* is submitted, this test is not sufficient. PHP will parse the *$id* variable as a string, and perform a comparison test with the ASCII values rather than numerical values. Since the ASCII value of 1 (the first character in the string) is greater than the ASCII value of 0 (which is also parsed as a string), the test will return true, and the subsequent commands will be executed. The following code is then executed:

```
UPDATE accounts SET password = 'qwerty' WHERE id =
    1254 or 1 = 1;
```

which will also modify every password in the table.

The right solution is to check that the $id variable is numeric:

```
if (is_numeric($id)) {
   $sql = "UPDATE accounts SET password = '".
      $password."' WHERE id = ".$id;
   (...)
}
```

If the *$id* variable is not a number, the query will not be executed. However, to avoid producing an SQL error if the $id variable is empty (empty variables are viewed as numeric), we should rewrite the test as follows:

```
if (is_numeric($id) && $id > 0) {
   (...)
}
```

We can clearly see that protecting against SQL injection is relatively simple, but highly tedious. It is easy to forget to perform a check, rendering the application vulnerable to attack.

The attack is only possible because the query is executed dynamically, i.e. because it is sent intact. The database server interprets it dynamically when it is executed.

If the query is transmitted in two parts, i.e. by first sending the code without the variables, then transferring an array with the values of these variables at the time of execution, there is no risk of injection. Passing variables in this way guarantees that they will be interpreted as is, and that they cannot modify the command being executed.

Here is a general diagram of this procedure:

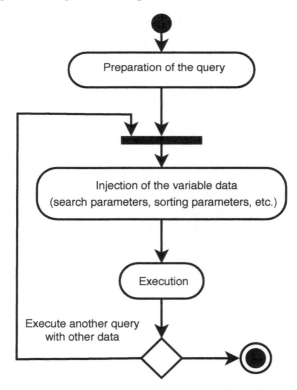

Figure 4.1. *General principle of prepared SQL queries*

Initially, a general version of the query code is sent to the database server, with question marks replacing the variables that will be needed to execute it later. The server prepares the request by calculating the optimal execution strategy.

The program then separately requests the execution of the query, sending the variables in an array. The server replaces the question marks with the contents of the variables, and executes the query.

If the same query is needed several times with different values, it can simply be re-executed by providing new data each time. The preparation phase is only performed once, which improves the efficiency and therefore the speed of execution of the server.

Since the query code is defined during the initial phase, there is no risk of injection: the query can no longer be modified by the content of the transmitted variables.

Below is an example based on PDO, a database access interface implemented in PHP (the same interface also exists for Java with JDBC). Consider again our earlier example of looking up an account. We begin by preparing the query, without specifying the search values, instead denoting the positions of the variables by question marks:

```
$sql = "SELECT id FROM accounts WHERE name = ? AND
    password = ?";
$pds = $db->prepare($sql);
```

$db is the database connection created by PDO. *$pds* is a *PDOStatement* object, one of the objects used by PDO. Note that the variables are replaced by question marks, and that they are not in quotes.

We then ask the database to execute the query by sending an array containing the arguments:

```
$data = array ($name, $password);
$pds->execute($data);
```

The query is no longer dynamically constructed and no longer depends on the submitted string; the values will be inserted into the query to replace the question marks.

If a variable that is expected to be numeric contains a string, the database will return an error: it checks the variable type when executing the code. The content of the variable doesn't matter: since it is no longer interpreted when the query is constructed, there is no risk that it will cause unintended instructions to be executed.

PDO allows us to replace the question marks with explicit variable names. In this case, we send an associative array at execution, i.e. an array that associates the values with the labels that they replace. Here is an example of this:

```
$sql = "SELECT id FROM accounts WHERE name = :
    login
AND password = :password";
$pds = $db->prepare($sql);
$data = array ("login"=>$name, "password"=>
    $password);
$pds->execute($data);
```

This makes the code easier to read, and is also compatible with the information sent by the browser (superglobal arrays such as $_POST and $_REQUEST);

This solution is usually the best way of preventing SQL injection attacks.

To conclude this section on code injection, we should remember that SQL is not the only vulnerable language: code can be injected into LDAP directory queries, XML files (using the XPath query syntax), etc. Injection can also be a concern when commands are allowed to be directly executed by the host system, for example with *bash* in Linux.

It would be tedious to attempt to list every possible case and every possible countermeasure. Many websites give explanations and security advice, e.g. for XML/XPATH [OWA 14c].

In most cases, protection involves escaping potentially dangerous characters, or using prepared statements wherever possible.

4.2.2. *Circumventing the login process and session hijacking*

The HTML protocol is a "stateless" protocol, which means that each request sent to the server is viewed as a new request. To keep track of users from page to page, applications use cookies, which are small files containing a session identifier that are stored in the browser.

If this identifier is stolen, attackers can impersonate legitimate users. Since wireless connections have become more widespread, this type of attack has unfortunately become more frequent. There also exist JavaScript scripts that attempt to steal cookies from other applications (other websites).

To protect against this, we must ensure that session cookies are only sent over encrypted connections. Furthermore, after each login and logout, a new session identifier should be generated. We must also ensure that sessions do not last too long, and that the cookie expires.

The example of code given below can be used to secure the session cookie.

First, the session is configured to operate in *strict* mode, which forces one unique identifier per session. The maximum inactivity period is set to 1 hour (3600 seconds).

```
$APP_session_ttl = 3600;
ini_set ( "session.use_strict_mode", true );
ini_set ( 'session.gc_probability', 1 );
ini_set ( 'session.gc_maxlifetime',
   $APP_session_ttl );
```

These commands are executed before beginning the session, which is manually created:

```
/**
 * Begin session
 */
@session_start ();
```

It is important to check that the session has not expired, but simply relying on the cookie is not sufficient. If nothing happens for longer than the chosen maximum period, the session is deleted using the *session_unset()* command, which deletes the session variables, and *session_destroy()*, which completes the deletion process. The time of last execution is stored in the *$_SESSION["lastActivity"]* variable.

```
/*
 * Check the session cookie and delete if
   necessary
 */
if (isset ( $_SESSION ['lastActivity'] ) && (time
   () - $_SESSION ['lastActivity'] >
   $APP_session_ttl)) {
   session_unset ();
   session_destroy ();
}
```

The exact time is saved to memory so that the session duration can be calculated later. If the session began longer ago than the chosen inactivity period, it is regenerated: a new identifier is created.

```
$_SESSION ['lastActivity'] = time ();
if (! isset ( $_SESSION ['created'] )) {
   $_SESSION ['created'] = time ();
} else if (time () - $_SESSION ['created'] >
   $APP_session_ttl) {
   /*
    * The session is older than the duration of
      the session cookie: regenerate cookie
    */
   session_regenerate_id ( true );
   $_SESSION ['created'] = time ();
}
```

Finally, this script ends by securing the session cookie, which is forced to take specific parameters (namely, *time () + $APP_session_ttl*, *https* protocol only - *$cookieParam ["secure"]*, *$cookieParam ["httponly"]*).

```
/*
 * Regenerate the session cookie
 */
```

```
$cookieParam = session_get_cookie_params ();
$cookieParam ["lifetime"] = $APP_session_ttl;
$cookieParam ["secure"] = true;
$cookieParam ["httponly"] = true;
setcookie ( session_name (), session_id (), time
    () + $APP_session_ttl, $cookieParam ["path"],
    $cookieParam ["domain"], $cookieParam ["secure
    "], $cookieParam ["httponly"] );
```

We can also check that the client IP address does not change during the session. This is not an absolute security measure (attackers can forge the address information shown to the application), but it adds an additional layer of difficulty. This can be done as follows:

```
/**
 * Check the session/IP address pair
 */
if (isset ( $_SESSION ["remoteIP"] )) {
    if ($_SESSION ["remoteIP"] !=
        getClientIPAddress()) {
        // Attempted session hijacking - close
            session
        session_unset ();
        session_destroy ();
    }
} else {
    $_SESSION ["remoteIP"] = getClientIPAddress();
}
```

This check uses a function that searches for the client's IP address, but which doesn't know whether the application is protected by a reverse-proxy server. Reverse-proxy servers are installed at the entrance to the company network to avoid leaving open a direct connection to the web server. The downside is that the IP address included natively in the *$_SERVER["REMOTE_ADDR"]* variable will always be the address of the reverse proxy: instead, we need to use a different variable defined specifically for this kind of situation:

```
function getClientIPAddress(){
```

```
/*
 * Determine whether the server is located
   behind a reverse proxy
 */
if (isset($_SERVER["HTTP_X_FORWARDED_FOR"])){
        return   $_SERVER["HTTP_X_FORWARDED_FOR
           "];
    /*
     * Normal case
     */
    }else if (isset ($_SERVER["REMOTE_ADDR"]))
       {
        return $_SERVER["REMOTE_ADDR"];
    } else
      return -1;
}
```

For these scripts to be effective, they must be executed each time that a page is requested.

4.2.3. *Executing code to redirect to another website, or Cross Site Scripting (XSS)*

This attack executes malicious code in the browser without the user's knowledge. It either redirects the user to a malicious website designed to look identical to the original website, or retrieves information that will allow the attacker to impersonate the user.

The attack exploits the fact that the browser can interpret the commands sent by the server either to display information (this is how HTML works) or to execute scripts. One of the simplest examples of this mechanism is that of a forum.

Suppose a poster adds the following text to a forum post:

```
<meta http-equiv="Refresh" content="0; url=http://
  www.maliciouswebsite.com/" >
```

This command tells the browser to refresh the page after 0 seconds, and specifies a new address to display. It is sometimes used to redirect users to a new website when the old site becomes obsolete.

In our case, when the browser displays the message, it will execute the command and redirect the user to the malicious website. Anybody who views the page containing this text will be redirected to the fake website.

In the HTML language, tags are used both to define the way that information is displayed and to execute code. These tags are enclosed by the characters < and >. Browsers read these tags and interpret their contents to determine how the webpage should be displayed.

To protect against this type of attack, we simply need to replace these tags with safe alternate characters. Thus, instead of sending the character < to the browser, it is better to send the string *<*, which will be displayed as the same symbol. This string will never be misinterpreted as executable code.

The PHP function *htmlspecialchars()* can be used to encode potentially problematic characters, including single and double quotes (' and "), less-than and greater-than symbols (< and >), and the ampersand (&).

The following function can encode an array of variables:

```
function encodehtml($data) {
    if (is_array ( $data )) {
        foreach ( $data as $key => $value ) {
            $data [$key] = encodehtml ( $value );
        }
    } else {
        $data = htmlspecialchars ( $data );
    }
    return $data;
}
```

This is a recursive function that can be applied to nested arrays.

Using SMARTY [SMA 16], a template plugin that can separate HTML code from PHP code, it is easy to encode all of the variables passed to the browser as follows:

```
foreach ( $smarty->getTemplateVars () as $key =>
   $value ) {
   if (in_array($key, array("menu", "message")) ==
      false) {
      $smarty->assign ( $key, encodehtml ( $value
         ) );
   }
}
```

This encodes all SMARTY variables, except for those contained in the array. In this example, the variables contain HTML tags that should be interpreted as such by the browser (the menu and the welcome message, which include line breaks).

Be careful not to save the encoded values in the database! If a data record contains:

```
if a < b, then...
```

and is saved with HTML encoding, then the content of the field in the database will be:

```
if a &lt; b, then...
```

When the page is next displayed, this creates a problem: the & character will be encoded. The text will be turned into:

```
if a &amp;lt; b, then...
```

Similarly, if the field is exported to a PDF file, or if native SQL queries are executed outside of the application, this can cause displayed text to contain mistakes.

To avoid this problem, the values sent by the browser need to be decoded before being processed by the application, using the *htmlspecialchars _decode()* command.

The following function performs this operation:

```
function decodehtml($data) {
```

```
if (is_array ( $data )) {
    foreach ( $data as $key => $value ) {
        $data [$key] = decodehtml ( $value );
    }
} else {
    $data = htmlspecialchars_decode ( $data );
}
return $data;
}
```

It should be called at the beginning of the script to transform each of the variables submitted by the GET or POST protocols:

```
$_GET = decodehtml($_GET);
$_POST = decodehtml($_POST);
```

4.2.4. *Insecure direct object references*

In some applications, giving a user access to a module gives that user access to all information managed by the module. This is not always a problem, but in some cases it can be undesirable. For example, in a banking site, each customer should only be able check their own account, and not their neighbors' accounts. The same is true for commercial websites, in which users' shopping carts should be invisible to everybody else.

If records are accessed from the browser by specifying the actual value of their key in the database, it can be tempting to try to manually modify this key to access other records. If there are no additional checks, this operation can allow unauthorized access to information.

There are two ways of combating this attack: the first is to verify that access to the given key is authorized each time that a record is requested. This approach is somewhat complicated, and requires a database call for each operation. It is however a valid approach when the key has a tangible representation (a number attached to a label, for example).

The second approach, which we shall study here, is to replace the true key with a recalculated key. Keys are rewritten before being sent to the browser, and a lookup array is created. When the browser sends data in return, the true key value is read from the array. If the submitted information cannot be found in the lookup array, the process is terminated.

In PHP, this mechanism is relatively simple to implement, although it requires some care when writing the pages that manage the interaction with the browser.

We start by creating a general-purpose class for managing the lookup array. We will need the following variables for this class:

```
class TranslateId {
    private $lookup;
    private $reverse_lookup;
    private $fieldname;
    private $counter = 1;
```

$lookup is an array with each entry corresponding to a real key value. *$reverse_lookup* is the reverse array, which allows us to find the value shown to the browser given the true key value.

$fieldname contains the name of the column containing the key in the array, and *$counter* is a counter used to generate the numbers sent to the browser.

The class constructor simply states the name of the key:

```
function __construct($fieldname) {
    if (strlen($fieldname) > 0)
        $this->fieldname = $fieldname;
}
```

We now require two functions. The first stores true key values and retrieves the number assigned by the class:

```
function setValue($dbId) {
    if ($dbId > 0) {
        if (! isset($this->reverse_lookup[$dbId])
        ) {
        $this->lookup [$this->counter] = $dbId;
        $this->reverse_lookup[$dbId] = $this->
            counter;
```

```
        $key = $this->counter;
        $this->counter ++;
        } else
          $key = $this->reverse_lookup[$dbId];
        return $key;
    }
  }
```

This function checks whether the key already exists in the reverse array (*$this->reverse_lookup*), if not, a new value is generated.

The second function performs the reverse operation, i.e. retrieves the real value of the key from the information given by the browser.

```
function getValue($id) {
    if ($id > 0) {
        $dbId = $this->lookup[$id];
        return $dbId;
    } else
        return 0;
}
```

Finally, the following function handles all keys for a set of records, for example a list of customer files:

```
function translateList($data) {
    /*
     * Translate each row of the array
     */
    foreach ( $data as $key => $value ) {
        if (isset ( $value [$this->fieldname   ]))
            {
            if (!isset($this->reverse_lookup[
                $value [ $this->fieldname ]]))
                $this->setValue($value[$this->
                    fieldname]);
            $data [$key] [$this->fieldname] =
                $this->reverse_lookup[$value [
                $this->fieldname ]];
```

```
        }
    }
    return $data;
}
```

The function takes a three-dimensional array as an input (one row per database record, each row containing the set of properties retrieved by the SQL query). *$value* is one row of the array.

It replaces the field containing the key with the value generated by the class, and updates the lookup array.

We will now implement this within our application. The class needs to be stored as a session variable so that the data is saved.

This small script, which must be executed for each page call, will initialize all of the translators required by the application.

```
$translators = array (
        "it_customer" => "customer_id",
        "it_order" => "order_id",
        "it_item" => "item_id");
foreach ( $translators as $key => $value ) {
    if (! isset ( $_SESSION [$key] ))
        $_SESSION [$key] = new TranslateId ( $value
            );
}
```

In this case, we have three translators to implement. The *$translators* array is indexed by the name of each translator, with values given by the names of the column containing the key in the array.

When information is sent to the browser, the keys are translated first:

```
$data = $_SESSION ["it_customer"]->translateList (
    $dataClass ->getListSearch ( $dataSearch ) );
```

In this example, the function *$dataClass->getListSearch* retrieves the list of information from *$dataSearch*, which is an array containing all of the search criteria.

Finally, after receiving information back from the browser, the reverse operation is performed to recover the true value of the key:

```
$data["customer_id"] = $_SESSION ["it_customer"]->
    getValue($data["customer_id"]);
```

Using a class such as the one above also protects against key-based SQL injection attacks: if the information submitted by the browser cannot be found in the lookup array, then the key is set to zero, at least in the example shown here.

4.2.5. *Poorly configured application or environment security*

During development, it is useful to configure error messages to display directly on the screen, allow browsing through directories, and access example files from third-party libraries. However, in production, all of these things must be disabled, default accounts should be deactivated or removed, etc.

Applications are often delivered with default settings, such as the login *admin* with password *password*. This makes the software easier to set up, but we must remember to delete them later.

We also need to ensure that the server and all of its components are up-to-date and do not have any known vulnerabilities.

The best way to do this is to apply formalized directives at the start of production that have been validated by the team responsible for operational security. This can also be done during pre-production, a phase in which a second platform identical to the production platform is set up to check that everything works properly (see section 7.1.4). We can also add instructions to the code to prevent certain information from being visible to users, as we discussed when we configured the Apache server (see section 3.5).

4.2.6. *Leaking sensitive information*

The application might handle personal information belonging to the user, such as credit card information. This information should never be accessible.

This kind of security failure can result from a lack of access control, although there can be other causes too.

Servers typically store events (errors, access, changes) in log files. If these log files are accessible, the information contained within them can be stolen.

To protect against this type of attack, we must first perform the crucial step of identifying sensitive data, so that we know what to protect. It is highly recommended to implement encryption at the system architecture level: databases containing sensitive information should be systematically encrypted. We must also remember to protect database backups, which can also potentially leak information if improperly secured.

The logging procedures (log files) should also be inspected to ensure that they do not reveal sensitive information, that they are correctly protected, and that the mechanisms or programs that access the logs are themselves properly secured.

Of course, these recommendations relate to system operations rather than programming as such. But some of these issues are directly relevant to developers.

The application will have access to a database, and therefore has a login and password. Sometimes, programmers forget to properly protect this information. For example, the database password might be accidentally stored in a file that is visible from the web, or placed in a forge (storage repository for code) accessible to others.

Therefore, it highly recommended to use different database access details for development and production.

There are several techniques for achieving adequate protection. The first is to conduct a review of active accounts prior to the start of production, i.e. inspect all identification details contained in the program or the database. If any of the information found by this review is unnecessary, or is still set to default values, it should be removed.

Furthermore, database connections should be made from a dedicated account that only has the permissions it actually requires, and which only works from the production server. With PostgreSQL, we can define accounts that are only authorized to connect from one specific address. To do this, we add instructions to the configuration file *pg_hba.cfg*. An example configuration is given below:

```
# ldaps identification, except for web
    applications
# connect in MD5 mode with the application account
# from the web server
host      all       all             10.33.1.25/32
    md5
# general case
host    all         all        10.33.2.0/24      ldap
    ldapserver=ldap.company.com ldapprefix="uid="
    ldapsuffix=",ou=people,dc=company,dc=com"
    ldaptls=1
```

The first line states that native-mode PostgreSQL identification, i.e. identification using a login and password generated by the database server, is only authorized from the address *10.33.1.25*, which is the address of the web server in this example.

Others can connect to the server using the company's *LDAP* login, provided that the IP address of their computer is located in the address block ranging from 10.33.2.0 to 10.33.2.254.

Access to the file containing this account must be protected by placing a *.htaccess* file (see section 3.5.6) that prevents users from directly browsing the folder in which it is located.

```
order deny,all
deny from all
```

Finally, the file must have a *.php* filetype to guarantee that it is interpreted and never displayed in cleartext if accessed directly by accident. This file could also be stored outside of the application file system, and accessed by loading it with the PHP functions for reading files.

Although this type of attack often targets web applications, the same problem is also extremely common with network equipment such as switches and embedded systems, which are deployed with default accounts and passwords. Users very often forget to change these defaults. Another common situation is that manufacturers include a privileged account with a unique password (or one that is easy to deduce[1]) to make things easier for maintenance teams. Once again, this is an example of unacceptable practice, due to the risks associated with leaking the password or the procedure for deducing it.

4.2.7. *Lack of access-level control for certain functions*

This attack primarily exploits poorly structured applications, which all too often rely on the principle of *security by obscurity*.

To make things easier for themselves, some programmers place the administrative pages of their website in a subfolder that can be accessed via a URL that is not referenced in their application. If attackers discover this URL, or if they deduce it by browsing the structure of the program, and if this page does not have any other protective measures, they will be able to impersonate the administrator.

We need to be especially careful with test pages. They are often created to test that a function works properly, then forgotten: they can reveal valuable information to attackers. Similarly, pages are often created to display the output of the *phpinfo()* command, which is useful for checking the configuration of the server. If the access rights to these pages are not properly managed, they can reveal the list of components and their versions in the production platform. This is never a good idea.

The solution is to ensure that access control applies to all pages of the application. Implementing MVC architecture (see Chapter 6) is probably the best way of doing this, as it creates a single point of entry. This makes it possible to systematically run verification scripts for each module of the software.

---

1 For example, one photocopier manufacturer uses part of the MAC address – the physical address of the network card – as the password.

4.2.8. *Tricking users into unknowingly running legitimate commands*

This attack is known as Cross Site Request Forgery (CRSF). The attackers attempt to trick users into unknowingly executing a modification request, for example by inserting it into an email, a *JavaScript* file, etc. By clicking on an image or a malicious link, the user triggers the operation. If the user is already logged in, the attack is highly likely to succeed: the attacker will have successfully tricked an authorized user into running code.

There are two methods for protecting against this type of attack. The first is to generate a unique token when sending entry forms, which is checked when the form is sent back to the server. This is usually the recommended approach, but it can be complicated to implement, as it might require every form in the application to be modified.

Cryptographic functions are perfect for generating tokens, since they guarantee that the tokens will be impossible to guess:

```
function generateToken() {
    global $view;
    $token = bin2hex(openssl_random_pseudo_bytes
        (64));
    $_SESSION["token"] = $token;
    $view->set($token, "token");
}
```

This function passes the token to the view (see section 6.2.2).

To verify that a page is not called from outside of its usual context of execution, we can simply check the token:

```
function verifyToken() {
    $return = false;
    if ($_REQUEST["token"] == $_SESSION["token])
        $return = true;
    // regenerate the token
    generateToken();
    return $return;
}
```

This function both checks the token and generates a new one.

The second method for protecting against this type of attack is to give a description of the application storyboard, i.e. the sequence in which events should be expected to occur. For example, the *personWrite* module, which writes information to the database, should only be executed if the previously executed module was *personChange*, which sent the form to the browser.

If the *personWrite* module is called but *personChange* was not the last module to be executed, the storyboard has been violated, which might indicate a CRSF attack.

Of course, attackers could attempt to call both pages successively, which would pass this test: single-use tokens are the only way to reliably counter the attack. Still, this kind of measure makes things more difficult for would-be attackers.

Storyboard checks are also useful for preventing accidental repetitions when creating entries. If a user saves a form, then presses the *F5* key to refresh, a new copy of the form will be sent to the server. But since this does not match the storyboard of the application (*personWrite* was called after *personWrite*), the software will know that the duplicate submission should be ignored.

Tokens also prevent this kind of behavior, since the token is regenerated each time that the page is called.

4.2.9. *Using components with known vulnerabilities*

If you use well-known frameworks, such as Symphony [SYM 15], you need to be sure to have the latest updates. Similarly, if you use third-party components, you should regularly check for new versions: there's a good chance that security issues will have been patched. Components created in the 2000s will not include recent technical developments, and are likely to contain vulnerabilities that were not well-understood at the time.

Attackers love to target these popular frameworks and components. If a vulnerability is discovered in one of them, the sheer number of affected websites is sufficient motivation to launch an attack.

To protect against this, we must review the components used by an application each time that the application is updated, and if necessary install the latest available versions of these components. Whenever possible, it is a good idea to subscribe to the mailing lists of these products to be informed of the latest news. Patched vulnerabilities are regularly announced, allowing you to be more reactive in the event of a problem.

4.2.10. *Refusing redirects*

Some web applications use redirects to display content from other websites. If these redirects can be dynamically modified by the user (for example by allowing them to choose the information displayed by a direct link), they must be verified before redirecting the user or displaying the requested information.

4.3. Other countermeasures

4.3.1. *Checking UTF-8 encoding*

In the early days of computing, characters were encoded in 7 bits, with 127 possible characters ($2^7 - 1$). This was perfectly sufficient for English, which does not have any accents and requires very few special characters.

However, accents soon needed to be included to support other European languages. The first 127 characters remained the same, but each language had to implement its own specific encoding. By increasing to 8-bit encoding, 255 characters were made available (2^8). The International Standards Organization (ISO) defined multiple sets for different European languages. For instance, ISO-8859-1 was used in France for a long time. It was replaced in the early 2000s by ISO-8859-15, which was designed to include a character representing the euro (€).

This was now good enough for Europeans, but other languages also required their own character sets: Arabic, Asian languages, and Slavic languages need more than just the Roman alphabet. Furthermore, for applications used by companies operating in several different countries, encodings based on ISO standards created problems.

The UTF-8 standard was therefore created to cover all cases. If a character can be represented by the original 127 character, it is stored in a byte. If not, it is stored in two bytes, allowing over 65,000 possible characters (2^{16}). This is enough to meet the needs of the whole world, and so UTF-8 was universally adopted.

However, returning to the perspective of security, some attackers began to craft sequences of characters that resemble UTF-8 but are not UTF-8, being either too long or malformed. These character sequences can trigger unintended operations.

To overcome this problem, it has now become necessary to check each character of both the variable names and values in browser-submitted requests. This can easily be done by adding the following code to the beginning of the script:

```
function check_encoding($data) {
    $result = true;
    if (is_array ( $data ) == true) {
        foreach ( $data as $key => $value ) {
            if (check_encoding ( $value ) == false ||
                check_encoding($key) == false)
                $result = false;
        }
    } else {
        if (strlen ( $data ) > 0) {
            if (mb_check_encoding ( $data , "UTF -8" )
                == false)
                $result = false;
        }
    }
    return $result;
}
```

This is a recursive function that can be used with *n*-dimensional arrays. It calls itself on each array-type value until it reaches non-array-type values. This function inspects not just the values, but the keys (*$key*) of each associative array.

It can be implemented in the controller:

```
if (check_encoding ( $_REQUEST ) == false) {
```

```
echo( "Character encoding error");
die;
}
```

If an encoding error is found, the application displays a message and terminates.

4.3.2. *Analyzing uploaded documents with an antivirus*

If an application allows users to upload documents to the server, it is highly advisable to check that they are virus-free before storing them.

For servers running Linux, this task can be entrusted to Clamav [CLA 15b], a widely used open-source antivirus.

Clamav should be available from the repository of any recent distribution. You can check that it is correctly installed by following the instructions given in this document: `https://wiki.archlinux.org/index.php/ClamAV` [CLA 15a].

There are two possible ways to analyze files. The first is to install a PHP module that loads on startup and is always available. The second is to conduct the analysis by running the command provided by Clamav, i.e. ask the operating system to perform the operation. This solution is more expensive in terms of processing time (the command is reinitialized each time), but is the only possible option if the module is not available for your version of PHP. For example, at the time of writing of this book, the *php-clamav* module is not available for PHP7.

4.3.2.1. *Analyzing with a complementary module*

In this section, we will use the PHP library *php-clamav*, which was developed specifically to interface with Clamav. First, we need to install the *php* development packages:

```
sudo apt-get install php5-dev
sudo apt-get install libclamav-dev
```

We then download *php-clamav* [SOU 14], and compile the module:

```
cd /tmp
tar xvzf php-clamav-0.15.8.tar.gz
cd php-clamav-0.15.8
phpize
./configure --with-clamav
make
```

Finally, we install the module in one of the folders of the server:

```
sudo mkdir -p /usr/local/lib/php5/extensions
sudo cp modules/clamav.so /usr/local/lib/php5/
    extensions/
```

Now, we edit the */etc/php5/apache2/php.ini* file, adding the following entry to the section *Dynamic Extensions*:

```
extension=/usr/local/lib/php5/extensions/clamav.so
```

Restart Apache:

```
sudo service apache2 restart
```

We need to test that PHP can successfully interface with Clamav. To do this, retrieve the test file:

```
wget -O- http://www.eicar.org/download/eicar.com.
    txt > /tmp/testvirus.txt
```

We now modify the file *phpclamav_test.php*, replacing the name of the test file with:

```
$file = "/tmp/testvirus.txt";
```

Copy the file *phpclamav_test.php* into one of the folders of the server, e.g.:

```
sudo cp phpclamav_test.php /var/www/html/
```

In the browser, run the test program:

```
http://localhost/phpclamav_test.php
```

The program should return the following information:

```
Functions available in the test extension :
cl_info
cl_scanfile
cl_engine
cl_pretcode
cl_version
cl_debug


ClamAV version 0.98.7 with 4078886 virus
   signatures loadedcl_info() return :
cl_version() return : 0.98.7
cl_pretcode(CL_CLEAN) return : virus not found
cl_pretcode(CL_VIRUS) return : virus found
Execution time : 6.89 seconds
File path : /tmp/testvirus.txt
Return code : virus found
Virus found name : Eicar-Test-Signature
```

The *phpinfo()* command should also include an entry for Clamav:

```
Clamav support enabled
php-clamav version    0.15.8
libclamav version 0.99.2
```

We will now see how to implement antivirus checks in a PHP program. Before storing the uploaded file, we add the following few lines:

```
$virus = false;
if (extension_loaded ( 'clamav' )) {
$retcode = cl_scanfile ( $file ["tmp_name"],
   $virusname );
if ($retcode == CL_VIRUS) {
$virus = true;
$error_text = $file ["name"] . " : " . cl_pretcode
   ( $retcode ) . ". Virus found name : " .
   $virusname;
echo $error_text;
```

```
}
}
if ($virus == false) {
/*
 * Continue executing
 */
```

This programs checks that the *clamav* extension is indeed available. If so, it starts scanning the file. If a virus is detected, it displays a message, otherwise it continues.

4.3.2.2. *Using the clamscan program*

The *clamscan* program is available once Clamav is installed. It can be used to scan files.

Here is an example of an application.

First, we create two PHP exceptions, one to manage the discovery of a virus, and another to check that the files exist (the *clamscan* program and the file being scanned):

```
class VirusException extends Exception {};
class FileException extends Exception {};
```

Now we simply need to create a function to initiate the scanning process:

```
function testScan($file) {
   echo "Scanning file $file<br>";
   $clamscan = "/usr/bin/clamscan";
   $clamscan_options = "-i --no-summary";
   if (file_exists ( $file )) {
      if (file_exists ( $clamscan )) {
         exec ( "$clamscan $clamscan_options $file
            ", $output );
         if (count ( $output ) > 0) {
            foreach ( $output as $value )
               $message .= $value . " ";
            throw new VirusException ( $message );
         }
```

```
         } else
            throw new FileException ( "clamscan not
                found" );
     } else
        throw new FileException ( "$file not found"
            );
}
```

The chosen options for *clamscan* hide the result of the scan (*no-summary*), and only show messages indicating that a virus was detected (*-i*).

This function can be used as follows:

```
$testfilename = "/tmp/eicar.com.txt";
try {
    testScan ( $testfilename );
    echo "No virus found in the file by Clamav<br
        >";
} catch ( FileException $f ) {

    echo $f->getMessage ()."<br>";
} catch ( VirusException $v ) {
    echo $v->getMessage ()."<br>";
} finally {
    echo "End of test";
}
```

We used the test file provided by Clamav, which tests that the antivirus is working properly. If so, the script produces the following result:

```
Scanning file /tmp/eicar.com.txt
/tmp/eicar.com.txt: Eicar-Test-Signature FOUND
End of test
```

4.3.2.3. *Combining both methods*

Scanning with the *clamav.so* module is faster than calling *clamscan*. Both methods can be combined to obtain an approach that works in all environments. Below, we give another version of the above function, modified so that it first attempts to call the *clamav.so* module, and then calls the *clamscan* function if the module was not found:

```php
function testScan($file) {
   echo "Scanning file $file<br>";
   if (file_exists ( $file )) {
      if (extension_loaded ( 'clamav' )) {
         /*
          * Test with clamav.so
          */
         echo "Scanning with clamav.so<br>";
         $retcode = cl_scanfile ( $file ["tmp_name
            "], $virusname );
         if ($retcode == CL_VIRUS) {
            $message = $file ["name"] . " : " .
               cl_pretcode ( $retcode ) . ". Virus
                  found name : " . $virusname;
            throw new VirusException ( $message );
         }
      } else {
         /*
          * Test with clamscan
          */
         $clamscan = "/usr/bin/clamscan";
         $clamscan_options = "-i --no-summary";
         echo "Scanning with clamscan<br>";
         if (file_exists ( $clamscan )) {
            exec ( "$clamscan $clamscan_options
               $file", $output );
            if (count ( $output ) > 0) {
               foreach ( $output as $value )
                  $message .= $value . " ";
               throw new VirusException ( $message
                  );
            }
         } else
            throw new FileException ( "clamscan
               not found" );
      }
   } else
```

```
throw new FileException ( "$file not found"
   );
}
```

This approach allows us to cover all cases, and is compatible with PHP versions both 5 and 7.

4.3.3. *Preventing the browser from storing the login and password*

Modern browsers allow users to store account details and passwords in a *virtual store*, which can be encrypted by a unique password. There are also ways for users to store all of their passwords in "digital vaults", avoiding the need to remember them.

In some critical applications, storing the password is strongly discouraged: in theory this should always be the case for banking applications, which use sophisticated techniques to prevent the password from being saved without the user's knowledge. Some attackers use keyloggers, and publicly available computers such as those proposed by cyber cafés might also be equipped with keyloggers.

If you want to prevent the password from being stored, you can disable field auto-completion using the following *html* command:

```
<input name="password" type="password"
   autocomplete="off">
```

Unfortunately, this is not enough: modern browsers ignore this field when storing passwords.

One solution is to define the input fields for the account name and password outside of the form, then transfer the information filled out by the user to the form before it is submitted to the server. This can be done in a few lines of JavaScript.

First, we prompt users to fill out the login and password in fields that are not contained within a form:

```
Login: <input name="login" id="login" maxlength
  ="32" required autofocus>
<br>
Password: <input name="password" id="password"
  type="password" autocomplete="off" required
  maxlength="32">
```

We then define a form with two hidden fields and a submit button:

```
<form id="theForm" method="POST" action="
  checkLogin.php">
<input type="hidden" id="hiddenUsername" name="
  login">
<input type="hidden" id="hiddenPassword" name="
  password">
 <input type="submit">
 </form>
```

We now simply need to write some JavaScript code that will be executed when the browser submits the form. This code uses *JQuery* [JQU 15] to retrieve objects from the HTML page:

```
<script>
  $("#theForm").submit(function() {
    $("#hiddenUsername").val($("#login").val());
    $("#hiddenPassword").val($("#password").val())
      ;
  });
```

We intercept the event triggered when the user presses the *Enter* key, which has *ASCII* value *13*:

```
  $("#login,#password").keypress(function(e) {
    if (e.which == 13) {
      $("#theForm").submit();
    }
  });
</script>
```

Now, when the user confirms their login and password, this information is sent to the form, which sends it to the server.

Since the original fields are separate from the form, browsers will not necessarily[2] be able to store this information.

Another increasingly popular method is to use two different pages, one to enter the login and one to enter the password.

This is the simplest way of preventing passwords from being automatically saved, since specialized programs automatically search for *hidden* fields.

Other approaches have also been implemented, especially by banking applications. Banking passwords are just numbers (usually 6 digits to guarantee a sufficient level of security), and if they are blocked the user has to contact their branch to resolve the issue.

The passwords are entered by clicking on numbers arranged in a grid. The numbers are located in different positions each time.

There are two ways of doing this: either the grid is generated by the server, and the client sends the location of the boxes (a bit like *battleships*, where each player indicates target coordinates: A4, B5...), or JavaScript is used to generate the grid and then return the chosen number. The first solution is more secure: even if the computer is compromised, it is impossible to know the code, since only the positions of each number are saved and transmitted to the server.

4.3.4. *Encrypting database access*

When writing software, the database and the web server are often hosted on the same server. This is often true if the programmer is working locally, i.e. if the web server and database are running on the programmer's computer. But it can also be the case when test platforms are implemented: performance and security considerations are not necessarily relevant at this stage, so it is not uncommon for all subsystems to be grouped together on the same machine.

When everything is managed locally, queries between the application and the database are confined within the platform: no information travels over the

---

2 Sadly, this is becoming less and less true.

network. In this context, there is no point encrypting the traffic between the two. With PostgreSQL, it is not even possible.

But when the application is launched into production, the infrastructure often becomes more complex, and the web server might be hosted on a different machine than the one hosting the database. In this case, information might need to travel over the network.

This might only happen within a restricted part of the network, meaning that encryption is slightly redundant. This is often the case for virtual servers, i.e. servers that are hosted in different environments but located on the same physical machine. Depending on the set-up, there is little risk that communications between the two servers can be intercepted.

However, in some cases, it is impossible to guarantee that communications are perfectly contained. This might be the case if the servers are hosted on different physical machines without a special network architecture to guarantee that communications are not leaked. If so, it is important to take special precautions to ensure that queries sent from the web server to the database are correctly encrypted.

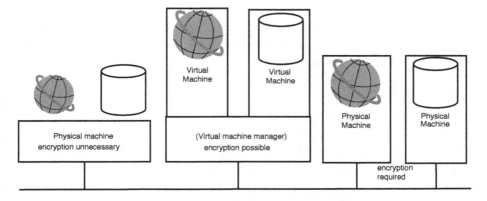

Figure 4.2. *When should communications between the web server and the database be encrypted?*

Today, database servers support encrypted connections. Some can even be configured to refuse unencrypted connections: this is often the case for interfaces that allow direct open read access, for example using remote access tools such as pgAdmin [PGA 14] for PostgreSQL.

4.3.4.1. *Enabling SSL support in PostgreSQL*

PostgreSQL has several parameters for configuring the encryption settings. These are available in the *postgresql.conf* file, which is usually located in the */etc/postgresql/9.5/main* folder. The most common are listed below:

```
ssl = true
#ssl_ciphers = 'HIGH:MEDIUM:+3DES:!aNULL'
ssl_cert_file = '/etc/ssl/certs/ssl-cert-snakeoil.
   pem'
ssl_key_file = '/etc/ssl/private/ssl-cert-snakeoil
   .key'
#ssl_ca_file = ''
#ssl_crl_file = ''
```

The first line enables encryption. The second (*ssl_ciphers*) specifies which protocols are accepted. The next three lines define the public and private keys that will be used, as well as the certificate of the certification authority (*ssl_ca_file*). Finally, the last line is used to specify the name of the certificate revocation list. This is the default server configuration: if you generated specific certificates, for example containing the name of the server, these parameters need to be updated (see section 3.2.3).

4.3.4.2. *Enabling SSL support in MySQL*

Unlike PostgreSQL, SSL support is not enabled by default in MySQL. To enable it, we need to modify the daemon configuration file (which is usually */etc/mysql/mysql.conf.d/mysqld.cnf*). Using the same certificates as for PostgreSQL, we simply need to change the following lines:

```
ssl-cert=/etc/ssl/certs/ssl-cert-snakeoil.pem
ssl-key=/etc/ssl/private/ssl-cert-snakeoil.key
```

We also need to check that the MySQL process can access the private key. You will probably need to run the following command to do this:

```
usermod -a -G ssl-cert mysql
```

4.3.4.3. *Activating encrypted connections with PDO*

It is increasingly common for interfaces to first attempt to connect to a database in encrypted mode and then switch to unencrypted mode if this is not available. For applications in production, it can be a good idea to force encryption and refuse all unprotected connections.

With PDO, the modern way of working with databases in PHP, this can be done by modifying the connection string. Here is an example for PostgreSQL:

```
$bdd = new PDO ("pgsql:host=server;dbname=database
   ;user=login;password=password;sslmode=
                require");
```

The *sslmode* option is the one that we need to configure. It can take several values:

– *prefer*: this indicates that the connection should be encrypted if encryption is supported by the server. This allows servers without encryption to be supported, for example in development platforms;

– *require*: this is the lowest level of forced encryption. Connections will only be opened in encrypted mode.

– *verify-ca*: the root certificate of the server is verified. This level can be used if the server has a self-signed certificate, i.e. a certificate that has not been validated by a certification authority;

– *verify-full*: the root certificate must be verified with a valid certification authority. This is the highest level of security possible, and all possible certificate checks are carried out.

In practice, the *require* level can be used to ensure that the connection is encrypted. The *verify-ca* requires the server certificate to be stored in a dedicated file, and prevents us from connecting to a rogue server that might be attempting to intervene. This is the level that should typically be used by applications with high risk levels.

The last level is only used in cases with a full security chain between the database server and the web server, with certificates validated by certification authorities.

4.4. Implementing a resource controller

If attackers manage to obtain access to a user's account, they can impersonate that user and attempt to perform a large number of operations to retrieve information or modify data. Similarly, if an employee loses their job but not their access, they might decide to delete or corrupt large amounts of information.

One way of minimizing the risk and detecting abnormal operations is to set up a resource controller. This controller is responsible for identifying any operations that are occurring excessively often, and, if necessary, shutting them down.

For example, if an account deletes more than 10 records per hour, it might be attempting to corrupt information. Similarly, more than 10 connection attempts in 10 minutes from the same IP address might indicate illegitimate activity. It might also be desirable to implement maximum daily allowances, etc.

From a practical point of view, implementing a resource controller is only viable if all modules and functions are managed from a single gateway. Again, MVC design principles (see Chapter 6). which advocate the usage of a single controller for managing rights and performing sequential operations, are probably the best solution for this: checks can be performed before initiating the requested actions.

Implementing this type of module is not free from side-effects: it is important to choose the thresholds carefully so that legitimate usage is not affected, e.g. legitimate requests might be blocked if the thresholds are set too low. The requested actions must also be uniquely identifiable, e.g. *getCustomerFile, putCustomerFile, delCustomerFile* to respectively display, update, or delete a customer file. Finally, all of the requested operations must be recorded and dated, so that they can be easily counted before they are executed.

This controller is given several tasks. Firstly, it analyzes user connections to check that the same account is not being used by multiple devices simultaneously. Secondly, it monitors the frequency with which certain functions are called. Returning to the above example, each time that the operator saves a customer file, this action is timestamped and logged. Finally, the controller implements a warning mechanism to alert both the operator and the operations managers, allowing them to respond appropriately.

4.4.1. *Managing user connections*

The simplest way of tracking user connections is to use a database table. Here is one possible example:

loginsession *Table of saved sessions*	
◆ loginsession_id	integer
● login	varchar
● login_date	timestamp
● session_id	varchar
○ last_request	timestamp
○ ip_address	varchar
● is_disconnect	boolean

Figure 4.3. *Structure of a table for tracking user sessions*

As well as the login and login date, the table contains other interesting information: the session number used by PHP, the client's IP address, and whether the session was manually terminated. Other information is also saved, such as information relating to the last few operations performed.

When the user logs in, it is easy to query this table to find any other connections that might still be active and which conflict with the current session. The SQL code below (encapsulated in PHP to manage the variables) gives an example.

```php
<?php
function getListSessionConcurrent($login) {
$ipaddress = getClientIPAddress() ;
$sessionId = session_id();
/*
 * Maximum lifetime of a session, in seconds
 */
```

```
$sessionMax = 86400;
/*
 * Maximum inactivity period, in seconds
 */
$sessionInactivity = 3600
}
$sql = " select login, login_date, last_request,
    ip_address from loginsession";
$where = " where login = '".$login/"'";
$where .= " and is_disconnect = false";
$where .= " and ip_address <> '".$ipaddress."'";
$where .= " and session_id <> '".$sessionId."'";
/*
 * Manage expiry dates
 */
$now = time();
$dateMaxStartSession = date('Y-M-d h:m:s', $now -
    $sessionMax);
$dateMaxLastRequest = date ('Y-M-d h:m:s', $now -
    $sessionInactivity);

$where .= " and login_date >= '".
    $dateMaxStartSession."'";
$where .= " and last_request >=  '".
    $dateMaxLastRequest."'";
/*
 * Execute the request
 */
return query_execute ($sql.$where);

}
?>
```

We need another function to find the client's IP address. This function is provided by the system, but in some cases we will need to account for the system architecture, e.g. if there is a server between the client and the web server (reverse-proxy server, used to improve the security of access to the internal network). We will reuse the function from before (see section 4.2.2):

```
function getClientIPAddress(){
(...)
}
```

We will also use the following function to execute the query:

```
function query_execute($sql) {
 /*
 * connect to the database
 */
$dsn = 'pgsql:dbname=database;host=127.0.0.1';
$user = 'dbuser';
$password = 'dbpass';
try {
   $dbh = new PDO($dsn, $user, $password);
   /*
   * Execute the request
   */
   return $dbh->execute ($sql);
} catch (PDOException $e) {
   echo  $e->getMessage();
}
}
```

This function tells us whether there are any other open sessions when the user logs in. If so, it is a good idea to inform the user of this, and offer an opportunity to close these other sessions.

Once the session identifier has been saved, it is relatively easy to delete it, at least server-side. There are two possible methods to do this. The first is to use an internal PHP function to delete the session:

```
public bool SessionHandler::destroy ( string
   $session_id )
```

which is easy to implement:

```
function destroy_other_session (string $session_id
   ) {
   /*
```

```
  * Check that the session being destroyed is
     not the active session
  */
if ($session_id != session_id()) {
    return SessionHandler::destroy ( $session_id
        );
} else
    return false;
}
```

The other solution is to directly delete the file containing the session. PHP stores sessions in separate files: if this file is deleted, the session is effectively destroyed too.

```
function destroy_other_session (string $session_id
    ) {
    $file = session_save_path()."/sess_".$id;
    if (file_exists($file)&& $session_id !=
    session_id()) {
        return unlink($file);
    } else
        return false;
}
```

4.4.2. *Monitoring behavior*

In this context, the objective can either be to identify or to block abnormal operation. For example, if a user modifies more than 10 files in one hour, the application can either block the account or send an alert to a monitoring unit.

To implement this check, we need to define alert criteria. Typically, we define multiple characteristic time periods: minimum processing time, number of operations per hour and per working day, for example.

These thresholds can be defined as follows:

```
$thresholds = array("module1"=>array(
    array (
        "type"=>"numMax",
```

```
        "number"=>10,
        "duration"=>3600
        ),
    array (
        "type"=>"numMax",
        "number"=>50,
        "duration"=>36000
        ),
    array (
        "type"=>"processingDuration",
        "before"=>"moduleXXX",
        "duration"=>120
        )
    ),
    "module2"=>array(
        . . .
    ),
    . . .
    );
;
```

For *module1*, we defined two thresholds for the number of customer files that can be processed within a given period of time. The first is triggered if more than 10 files are processed in one hour (times are expressed in seconds), and the second is triggered if more than 50 are processed in one working day (10 hours). The final threshold defines the minimum requirements for module sequences (e.g. display the input screen, then submit).

These thresholds should be defined by collaborating with the project managers to reflect the realistic operating conditions of the application.

Here, they were given in the form of a PHP array, but they could also be written as JSON or XML files.

We need to record all modules called by the user by adding another table:

module_call
Table of called modules

◆module_call_id	int
○login	varchar
○session_id	varchar
●module_name	varchar
●module_time	timestamp
●error_code	int

Figure 4.4. *Structure of a table for recording which modules are called*

As well as the login and the session identifier, this table contains the name of the called module, as well as the exact time that it was called.

There is one other column: *error_code*. If this has value 0, no error was detected, and the action was completed. If it has any other value, a threshold was triggered, and the action was blocked.

The error codes could be chosen to be the same as for HTML requests [WIK 15f]. For example, code 429 (too many requests) would give an informative description of the check that was performed.

With this structure, only a few SQL queries are needed to find the number of modules called within a certain period of time. Here is an example:

```
function getNumCallsFromModule(string $module,
    string $login, $duration) {
    $dateTest = date('Y-M-d h:m:s', time() -
        $duration);
    $sql = 'select count(*) as "number" from
        module_call';
    $where = " where module_name = :module";
    $where .= " and login = :login";
    $where .= " and module_time > :dateTest::
        datetime';
    $data = array("module"=>$module, "login"=>
        $login, "dateTest"=>$dateTest);
    try {
        $insertStmt = $this->dbh->prepare ($sql.
            $where);
```

```
        return $insertStmt ->execute ($data);
    }catch (PDOException $e) {
        echo $e->getMessage ();
        return false;
    }
}
```

This function could just as easily be used to test the number of times that a module was called within a given period or to check whether two modules were requested too quickly one after the other. This can be done simply by checking whether the previous module was requested more recently than the minimum period: if at least one record is found, the processing time is too low.

The following function adds a record to the *actionlog* table:

```
function actionlogAdd ($data) {
    $sql = "insert into module_call
        ( login , session_id , module_name ,
            module_time , error_code)
        values
        (: login , : session_id , : module_name , :
            module_time , : error_code)";
    try {
        $insertStmt = $this ->dbh ->prepare ($sql);
        $data ["session_id"] = session_id ();
        return $insertStmt ->execute ($data);
    }catch (PDOException $e) {
        echo $e->getMessage ();
        return false;
    }
    }
}
```

We still need to write a function to confirm that a module can be called:

```
function testModule ($module , $login) {
    global $thresholds;
    $error = 0;
    /*
```

```
 * Check whether the maximum number of calls
   has been exceeded
*/
foreach ($thresholds[$module] as $key=>$value)
     {
if ($value["type"] == "numMax") {
  $num = getNumCallsFromModule($module, $login
  , $value["duration"]);
  if ($num > $value["number"])
     $error = 429;
}
if ($value["type"] == "processingDuration") {
    $num = getNumCallsFromModule($value["
       before"], $login, $value["duration"]);
    if ($num > 0) {
       $error = 403;
    }
}
/*
 * Write the result
 */
$data = array (
        "login"=>$login,
        "module_name"=>$module,
        "module_time"=>date("Y-M-d H:i:s"),
        "error_code"=>$error;
actionlogAdd($data);
return $error;


}
```

We can simply call this final function to know whether the requested module should be executed effectively:

```
if (testModule($module, $login) == 0) {
   /*
    * processing
    */
   (...)
}
```

4.4.3. *Managing alerts*

Resource controllers are often implemented because the application they are monitoring is associated with a significant level of risk.

Simply prohibiting certain behavior is not enough: undesirable behavior needs to be identified and dealt with. Repeatedly blocking tasks performed too quickly might indicate an attempted attack. This attack should be handled quickly to prevent it from succeeding in its goal.

This type of information is often described as *weak signals*, i.e. clues that could easily go unnoticed but which are in fact signs of a much larger attack than expected.

There are two possible approaches to triggering alerts. The first is to immediately report any unusual events, for example by sending an email.

This can be effective, but soon becomes very difficult to manage if the thresholds are too sensitive: the teams receiving the alerts will eventually stop paying attention to them or will forget them.

The second solution is to automatically generate a log that is aggregated with other company logs. Specialized software can then be used to conduct a global analysis and identify more subtle behavior (account login associated with a blocked operation and messaging request performed within the same unit of time, for example).

These kind of logs can be generated using the *Syslog* tool[3] available with PHP:

---

3 Syslog is a system log management program included with all distributions of Linux. It uses a rotating procedure that compresses older files or eventually deletes them after a certain specified retention period.

In modern organizations, additional tools are installed to send the logs generated by each server to a central server. Several such tools exist, but RSYSLOG is one of the best-known examples [RSY 16].

Implementing this kind of platform is complex, but these analysis tools allow all operations performed by a single device to be monitored. Example implementations are available online [QUI 12].

```php
<?php
$dt = new DateTime();
$date = $dt->format("D M d H:i:s.u Y");
$app = "myApp";
$pid = getmypid();
$code_error = "$app message";
$level = "notice";
$message = "Log message";
openlog("[$date] [$app:$level] [pid $pid]
    $code_error",LOG_PERROR , LOG_LOCAL7);
syslog(LOG_NOTICE , "$message");
closelog();
?>
```

The *openlog()* function creates a record beginning with the date, formatted according to Apache notation. It also includes the process ID (PID) and an error code.

This string is followed by a colon, then the text contained in the *$message* variable. This is saved to the log file using the *syslog()* function.

The following text gives an example of how this would appear in the */var/log/apache2/error.log* file:

```
[Tue Jun 14 15:52:54.000000 2016] [myApp:notice] [
    pid 8069] myApp message: Log message
```

These logs can be collected using appropriate tools and then analyzed together.

The format needs to be standardized: log management tools such as RSYSLOG require properly formatted entries in order to be able to analyze them. The example shown above is identical to the error messages generated by Apache, and so can be directly processed by this kind of software.

There are also classes that can send the logs directly to a remote server using the RSYSLOG protocol. One of the most complete examples of such a class is given by *php.syslog.class* [LEI 13].

Managing User Logins
and Assigning Permissions

5.1. Managing user logins

Logging users is an essential part of any management application. This enables them to be assigned module access permissions (read and write). Access permissions are generally assigned using groups. Each user can be a member of one or several groups.

The first step is to verify that the person logging is indeed who they claim to be. The simplest mechanism for achieving this is to use login accounts and passwords. This login can be application-specific, but companies often prefer to use a centralized user database. This prevents employees from having to remember a different password for each application. Furthermore, when employees stop working at the company, it is easier to disable their accounts, and close their access to all software in a single operation.

Recently, as the Internet has grown, it has become customary for customers to log in with their email address. This has several advantages, such as the ability to send a password reset link if a user loses access to his/her account. Also, email addresses are necessarily unique, so two different users cannot have the same login.

There are other methods for identifying users. In some systems, personal digital certificates generated by the system are preferred. This guarantees that the user is properly identified: official identification is required when handing over the certificate. In these cases, we say that the user has been authenticated: not only is the user's account known, but his or her identity has been verified.

These certificates are currently viewed as highly secure, because they are based on asymmetric encryption, as we discussed earlier (see section 3.2.3). They can also be integrated into smart cards or encrypted USB keys, which further limit the risks of theft. However, this requires the implementation of very specific verification protocols, either based on reading the certificate stored in the browser, or installing a smart card reader, etc. This is typically makes things more difficult for technical support teams, who must help the users to correctly operate these devices.

If we restrict ourselves to login approaches based on *login/password*, three main approaches are generally used today to store account information: storing information in a database, querying the corporate directory, usually using the LDAP protocol (*Lightweight Directory Access Protocol*, a standard for managing directories [WIK 15e]) or outsourcing the login process to a specialized server, the CAS server (*Common Access Service*), which we will study in detail below.

The procedures for verifying personal certificates are typically integrated into the CAS servers, due to the complexity of their implementations and the security environment required to guarantee that the platform is reliable.

5.1.1. *Managing accounts in a database*

The first method is to store users in a database and directly generate their passwords in the application. This is the simplest procedure to design, but is nonetheless difficult to implement due to the risks associated with password storage.

Since computing power is continuously increasing[1], the risk that a given password can be broken is also steadily rising. A few years ago, passwords were required to have at least eight characters chosen from three of four character sets (numbers, lowercase, uppercase and special characters). Today, they need to have at least 12 characters chosen from all four available

---

1 Moore, an engineer at IBM, predicted that the computing power of processors will double every 18 months [WIK 15g].

character sets in order to rule out brute force cracking. This is only true if the number of authorized attempts is unlimited.

A password is considered to be good if the chance of it being guessed is smaller than $1/2^{11}$ (1 in 2048). A PIN code with four digits and three authorized attempts (after which the system is locked) meets this criterion: this is why the PIN codes used by banking cards are considered to be secure.

Without going into the full detail of a perfectly secure implementation, here is a list of key aspects that need to be ensured:

– the password must be encrypted using a hash function (see section 3.2.2), and it must be salted, i.e. associated with another piece of data to ensure that if two people choose identical passwords, they will still produce different hashes. If the list of passwords is leaked, this will make it more difficult for attackers to identify commonly used passwords;

– the procedure for changing passwords must impose some complexity on the choice of password. Typically, it is recommended to impose a minimum length of eight characters chosen from three of the four possible character sets: uppercase letters, lowercase letters, number and special characters;

– it should not be possible for the same password to be reused, and passwords should have a finite lifespan. This is rarely enforced for applications intended to be used by the general public or customers from outside of the company. Even banking websites do not require the password to be changed;

– if an automatic password recovery procedure is available for lost passwords, it should send an email with an encoded single-usage and time-restricted link that allows users to change their password on a dedicated page.

5.1.1.1. *Password reinitialization*

Below is an example of a scenario that can be implemented to reset a lost password (Figure 5.1).

The token should be generated using a cryptographic function to ensure that it cannot be guessed. It should not have an excessively long lifetime: usually, it should expire after 3 days, but this period can be reduced further.

To store the renewal token, we need a dedicated table in our database (Figure 5.2).

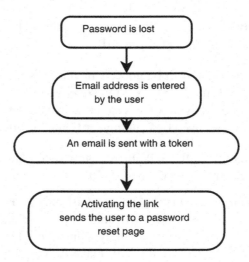

Figure 5.1. *Sequence of operations to reset a password*

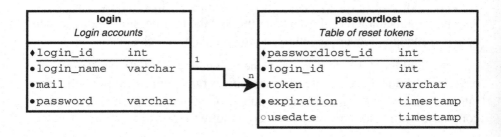

Figure 5.2. *Table used to store password reset tokens*

The *passwordlost* table stores the token, its expiration date and usage date. We need some functions to manage the password reset process.

The first function generates the token. We will reuse the code from earlier that we used to generate a token for protecting against *Cross Site Request Forgery* attacks (see section 4.2.8):

```
function generateToken() {
    return bin2hex(openssl_random_pseudo_bytes(64))
        ;
}
```

The second function stores the token in the table.

```
function setToken ($email) {
   /*
    * Find the login from the email
    */
   $login_id = getLoginFromEmail($email) ;
   $token = generateToken();
   try {
      if (createTokenForRecoveryPassword($login_id
         , $token)) {
         return $token;
      } else
         return false;
   } catch (Exception $e) {
      return false;
   }
}
```

This function creates the recovery token from the email provided by the user and stores it in the database. The *getLoginFromEmail()* function simply queries the database, which returns the identifier of the login record. If the login is not an email address, a consistency check can be included here by adding an argument. The function would then be called as follows:

```
$login_id = getLoginFromEmail($email, $login);
```

We will now create a function to store the token. This is entirely straightforward, as we simply need to calculate the expiration date:

```
function createTokenForRecoveryPassword($login_id,
      $token) {
   global $db;
   $token_duration = 259200; // 3 days, in seconds
   $sql = "insert into passwordlost(login_id,
      token, expiration)
         values (:login_id, :token, :expiration)";
   $data["login_id"] = $login_id;
   $data["token"] = $token;
```

```
$data["expiration"] = date("Y-m-d H:i:s", time
    () + $token_duration);
try {
    $insertStmt = $db->prepare ($sql);
    $insertStmt->execute($data);
    return true;
}catch (PDOException $e) {
    echo $e->getMessage();
    return false;
}
}
```

This function uses a PDO connection (*$db*) that needs to have been previously initialized.

The token is sent by email:

```
$crlf = "\r\n";
$token = setToken($email);
if (!$token == false){
    $subject = "Application XXX - password reset";
    $address = "https://myapp/passwordlost.php?
        token=$token&email=$email";
    $body=    "You requested a password reset.$crlf
              To do this, please copy the following
                 link into your browser:$crlf
              $address.$crlf
              This link will expire after 3 days.
                 $crlf
              If you did not request a password
                 reset,
              please ignore this message";
    mail ($email, $subject, $message);
}
```

The *passwordlost.php* script will need to check the token:

```
function tokenPasswordLostVerify($email, $token) {
    global $db;
```

```
$sql = "select passwordlost_id
from passwordlost
join login using (login_id)
where email = :email
and token = :token
and expiration < :expiration
and usedate is null";
$data["email"] = $email;
$data["token"] = $token;
$data["expiration"] = date("Y-m-d H:i:s");
try {
    $insertStmt = $db->prepare ($sql);
    $stmt->execute($data);
    return $stmt->fetchColumn();
}catch (PDOException $e) {
    echo $e->getMessage();
    return false;
}
}
```

The function sends a simple SQL query to the database, and returns the key of the *passwordlost* table. The script checks that the email address matches and that the token has not already been used (column *usedate* should have value null).

It needs to be run twice: once before displaying the page for entering the new password, and once after the form has been submitted, to check that the token is still valid.

Once the password was changed, we need to remember to update the record with the use date:

```
function setUsedate($passwordlost_id){
    global $db;
    $usedate = date('Y-m-d H:i:s');
    $sql = "update passwordlost set usedate = '".
        $usedate."'
            where passwordlost_id = :passwordlost_id
    ";
```

```
try {
    return $db->execute($sql);
}catch (PDOexception $e) {
    echo $e->getMessage();
    return false;
  }
}
```

This prevents the token from being reused, since the *usedate* column is no longer null.

This implementation must be perfectly mastered, and in particular all operations must be recorded (reset requests, whether or not the token was successfully used, etc.). This will make it easier to detect potentially fraudulent attempts (see section 4.4).

This mechanism is commonly used by commercial websites, which identify customers by their email address. It is rarely used in companies that rely on a central directory for identification, unless external users from outside of the company need to login.

5.1.1.2. *Enforcing password complexity*

Before storing a password in a database, we need to check its length and complexity. This check can be done using JavaScript in the browser, but as always, should be repeated by the server.

We can prevent the form from being submitted to the server if it contains invalid information by adding a test into the HTML page. To do this, we need the following JavaScript functions:

```
<script>
/*
 * tests whether the character is a punctuation
   symbol
 */
function checkPunc(num) {
    if (((num >= 33) && (num <= 47)) || ((num >=
        58) && (num <= 64))) {
        return true;
```

```
    }
    if (((num >= 91) && (num <= 96)) || ((num >=
        123) && (num <= 126))) {
        return true;
    }
    return false;
}
/*
 * tests whether the character is numeric
 */
function checkNumbers(num) {
    if ((num >= 48) && (num <= 57)) {
        return true;
    } else {
        return false;
    }
}
/*
 * tests whether the character is an uppercase
    letter
 */
function checkUppercase(num) {
    if ((num >= 65) && (num <= 90)) {
        return true;
    } else {
        return false;
    }
}
/*
 * Function called by the form to check
 * the password complexity
 */
function verifyComplexity(password) {
    var character = "";
    var isLower = 0;
    var isUpper = 0;
    var isPunctuation = 0;
    var isNumber = 0;
```

```
//console.log("password :" + password);
for (i = 0; i < password.length; i++) {
   character = password.substr(i, 1).charCodeAt
      (0);
   //console.log(i + " : " + character);
   if (checkUppercase(character)) {
      isUpper = 1;
   } else if (checkNumbers(character)) {
      isNumber = 1;
   } else if (checkPunc(character)) {
      isPunctuation = 1;
   } else
      isLower = 1;
}
var complexity = parseInt(isLower) + parseInt(
   isUpper) + parseInt(isPunctuation) +
   parseInt(isNumber);
if (complexity > 2) {
   return true;
} else
   return false;
}
/*
 * Check password length (8 characters minimum)
 */
function verifyLength(password) {
   if (password.length < 8) {
      return false;
   } else {
      return true;
   }
}
}
</script>
```

An example of form validation is given below. The password input fields have ids *pass1* and *pass2*, and error messages are displayed in *<div id="message"></div>* tags:

```
<script>
$(document).ready(function() {
   $("#form").submit(function (event) {
       var error = false;
       var message = "";
       /*
        * Checks
        */
       var pw1 = $("#pass1").val();
       var pw2 = $("#pass2").val();
       if (pw1 != pw2) {
          error = true;
          message = "Passwords do not match";
       } else if (verifyLength(pw1) == false) {
          error = true;
          message = "Password too short";
       } else if (verifyComplexity(pw1) == false)
          {
          error = true;
          message = "Password insufficiently
             complex";
       }
       $("#message").text(message);
       /*
        * Prevent form submission
        */
       if (error == true)
          event.preventDefault();
   });

});
</script>
```

Since everything that is performed browser-side must be checked, these
tests should also be reimplemented server-side. The following scripts repeat
the complexity check in PHP using a slightly different algorithm (in JavaScript,
the characters were evaluated using their ASCII numbers, whereas the PHP
script uses regular expressions):

```
function checkComplexity($password) {
    $long = strlen ( $password );
    $type = array (
            "lower" => 0,
            "upper" => 0,
            "number" => 0,
            "other" => 0
    );
    for($i = 0; $i < $long; $i ++) {
        $char = substr ( $password, $i, 1 );
        if ($type ["lower"] == 0)
            $type ["lower"] = preg_match ( "/[a-z
                ]/", $char );
        if ($type ["upper"] == 0)
            $type ["upper"] = preg_match ( "/[A-Z
                ]/", $char );
        if ($type ["number"] == 0)
            $type ["number"] = preg_match (
                "/[0-9]/", $char );
        if ($type ["other"] == 0)
            $type ["other"] = preg_match ( "/[^0-9
                a-zA-Z]/", $char );
    }
    $complexity = $type ["lower"] + $type ["
        upper"] + $type ["number"] + $type ["
        other"];
    return $complexity;
}
```

This script searches for different character sets within the password, using regular expressions to check for each character. The number returned by the *$complexity* variable is the total number of sets used in the password. This value can be analyzed to determine whether the password is sufficiently complex.

The full test given below checks both the length and the complexity of the password:

```
$passwordOk = false;
if (strlen($password)>= 8) {
   if checkComplexity($password) >= 3 {
      $passwordOk = true;
   }
}
if ( $passwordOk ) {
   /*
    * continue processing
    */
}
```

We can also implement other tests, for example to check whether the password is contained in a list of common words (a dictionary), or whether it contains part of the user's first name, last name or account details.

5.1.2. *Locking passwords*

To prevent attackers from conducting an exhaustive password search, we can lock the password after several unsuccessful attempts. However, attackers might simply test a few combinations and then wait for the user to re-enter the correct password, which will reset the number of authorized attempts. If the password is locked after 10 unsuccessful attempts, attackers can test 5–9 unique combinations daily, given the reasonable assumption that the user will enter the correct password at least once per day. By testing a few carefully chosen passwords each day, if the basic password complexity rules are not followed, attackers are likely to find the right one in a matter of weeks.

Login systems typically offer one of two types of locking: permanent locking and time-locking.

With permanent locking, brute-force password searching is essentially impossible, especially if the password is not contained in the list of most common passwords. However, this can create the risk of "denial of service": an attacker might decide to lock all passwords, including administrator passwords, to deny access to the system and impede the proper operation of the infrastructure under attack.

However, time-based unlocking makes brute-force password searching easier: if the password is unlocked after 10 min, an attacker can test 60 passwords per hour, or 250,000 attempts in 6 months. Again, if the password is complex, it is unlikely that it will be discovered. But if it can be easily deduced (child's name + number, for example, or switching lowercase and uppercase letters), the probability that it will be found increases strongly. One good way of detecting this type of attack is to track all instances of password locking and implement a mechanism that reports them.

If the same password is regularly blocked, this might indicate that an attempted intrusion is underway.

5.1.3. *Retrieving the login from the company directory*

Companies usually maintain a directory of their employees, which they use to log in when working on their computers (Windows sessions). In most cases, this directory is compatible with the LDAP standard [WIK 15e]. Some companies also set up their own directories based on open-source products such as *OpenLDAP* [OPE 15].

Delegating the identification process to the LDAP directory removes the need to manage password generation procedures and security measures. The mechanisms integrated into LDAP are instead responsible for these aspects.

The application simply needs to attempt to connect to the directory using the user's account and password in order to validate it.

The following example script performs this validation.

We begin by defining the directory connection settings:

```
function testLoginLdap($login, $password) {
    $LDAP_address = "localhost";
    $LDAP_port = 389;
    $LDAP_basedn = "ou=people,ou=example,o=company,
        c=com";
    $LDAP_user_attrib = "uid";
    $LDAP_v3 = true;
    $LDAP_tls = false;
```

These parameters include the IP address of the directory, the connection port (389 for unencrypted mode, 636 otherwise), the account search path in the directory (*$LDAP_basedn*), and the attribute of the record containing the login value (*$LDAP_user_attrib*). Nowadays, version 3 is always used. The last variable states whether or not the connection is encrypted, separately from the port number (in this example, it is not). In practice, it should not be possible to open an unencrypted connection unless the directory is hosted on the same machine as the web server (see section 4.3.4).

The connection test is only launched if the login and password have been populated:

```
if (strlen ( $login ) > 0 && strlen ( $password
    ) > 0) {
```

The login is transcoded to prevent LDAP injection attacks:

```
/*
 * transcode login to avoid LDAP injection
 */
$login = str_replace(array('\\', '*', '(',
    ')'), array('\5c', '\2a', '\28', '\29'),
    $login);
for ($i = 0; $i<strlen($login); $i++) {
    $char = substr($login, $i, 1);
    if (ord($char)<32) {
        $hex = dechex(ord($char));
        if (strlen($hex) == 1) $hex = '0' .
            $hex;
        $login = str_replace($char, '\\' .
            $hex, $login);
    }
}
```

Initialize the connection to the directory:

```
/*
 * Connect to the directory
 */
```

```
    $ldap = @ldap_connect ( $LDAP_address ,
        $LDAP_port ) or die ( "Connection to LDAP
        server failed." );
    if ($LDAP_v3) {
        ldap_set_option ( $ldap ,
            LDAP_OPT_PROTOCOL_VERSION , 3 );
    }
    if ($LDAP_tls) {
        ldap_start_tls ( $ldap );
    }
```

Finally, test the connection:

```
    $dn = $LDAP_user_attrib . "=" . $login . ","
        . $LDAP_basedn;
    /*
     * Attempt to connect with the user's login
        and password
     */
    $rep = ldap_bind ( $ldap , $dn , $password );
    if ($rep == 1) {
        return $login;
    }
    }
    return -1;
}
```

If the connection succeeds, i.e. if the value returned is greater than −1, then the user was successfully identified by the directory.

Connections to the LDAP directory are usually encrypted using the LDAPS protocol (*LDAP over SSL/TLS*). In this case, the connections uses port 636, which requires us to change the access settings:

```
$LDAP_tls = true;
$LDAP_port = 636;
```

5.1.4. *Delegating the login process to a CAS server*

The major disadvantage of using a database or an LDAP directory for login is that the application sees the *login/password* pair submitted by the user. This is not necessarily reassuring for the user: the user does not know the application code and cannot know whether the programmer stores this information in a hidden file for personal usage. Nor is the user necessarily awares the security measures that have been implemented. Users might have legitimate doubts about trusting the application with their password. Unfortunately, it is still all too common to encounter websites that send passwords by email: at the very least, this tells us that they do not take security seriously.

To avoid this problem, large companies and administrations can implement a unique login server shared by all applications. Each time that an application needs to know the identity of the user, it delegates the account verification process.

These login servers are described as CAS servers: *Common Access Service*.

We will see how this type of login procedure works.

5.1.4.1. *The principle of CAS*

The user requests access to an application (1) (Figure 5.3):

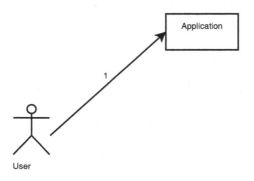

Figure 5.3. *The user requests access to an application*

The application does not know the user. It redirects the user's browser to the CAS server (2) (Figure 5.4):

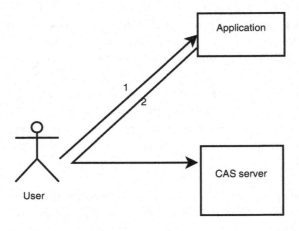

Figure 5.4. *The browser is redirected to the CAS server*

The CAS server does not know the user either. It opens a dialogue with the user to retrieve a username and password (3) (Figure 5.5):

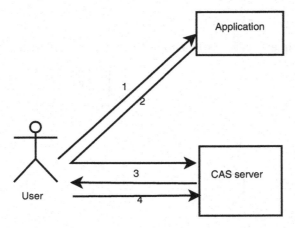

Figure 5.5. *The user enters his or her password*

The user submits his/her login and password (or presents a digital certificate, or a smart card, etc.) (4). The identification server uses its own directory to check that the user is indeed known and still has a valid account (5) (Figure 5.6):

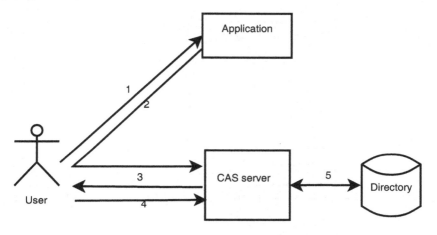

Figure 5.6. *The CAS server validates the login*

The CAS recognizes the user and redirects him/her to the application. In the redirect link, it indicates that it has validated the account by providing a unique ticket number (6) (Figure 5.7).

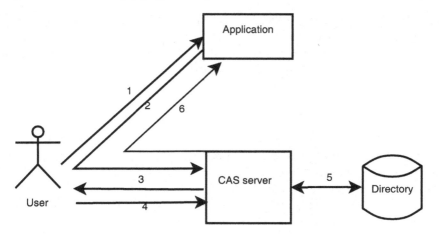

Figure 5.7. *The CAS server redirects the browser to the application*

The application retrieves the ticket number and checks it with the CAS server (7) (Figure 5.8). The login server returns a file with the user's login.

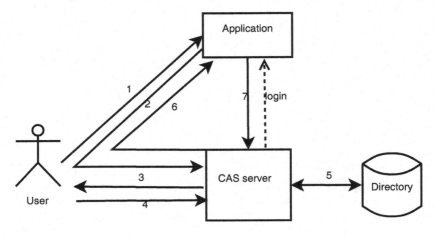

Figure 5.8. *The application retrieves the login from the CAS server*

Using this mechanism, the user can log into the application without having to reveal confidential information to it (password or other information). The CAS server acts as a trusted third party.

Suppose now the user wishes to connect to another application whose login process is also managed by the CAS server. At first, this other application does not know the user. The first steps (8 and 9) (Figure 5.9) are identical to those of the first connection (1 and 2): the application redirects the browser to the CAS server.

This is where the mechanism becomes interesting: the CAS knows the user, who has already logged in once. Rather than requiring the user to repeat the login process, it simply redirects the browser to the second application with a new ticket (10) (Figure 5.10).

The application simply needs to query the CAS server by sending the ticket number to retrieve the login (11) (Figure 5.11).

Users only have to log in once, and provided that they do not close their browser and the CAS server session does not expire, they can switch between applications without needing to repeat the login process.

This mechanism is often known as *SSO (single sign-on)*.

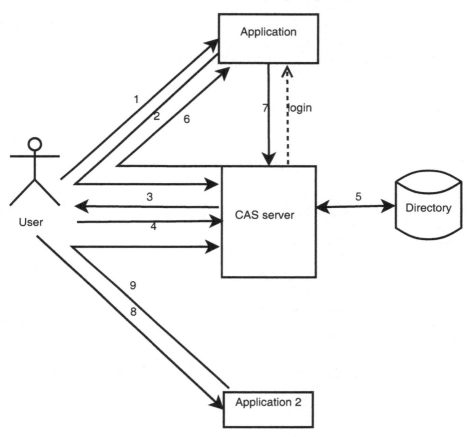

Figure 5.9. *The user connects to a new application*

5.1.4.2. *Implementing a CAS server-based login process*

We will now see how this functionality can be implemented in our application code. The phpCAS client may be downloaded from the project website [JAS 15]. We then simply need to insert a few lines into the code:

```
if (!isset($_SESSION["login"] {
    $CAS_plugin = 'CAS-1.3.3/CAS.php';
    $CAS_address = "https://server/CAS";
    $CAS_port = 443;
```

```
include_once ($CAS_plugin);
phpCAS::client ( CAS_VERSION_2_0, $CAS_address,
    $CAS_port, $CAS_uri );
phpCAS::forceAuthentication ();
$_SESSION ["login"] = phpCAS::getUser ();
}
```

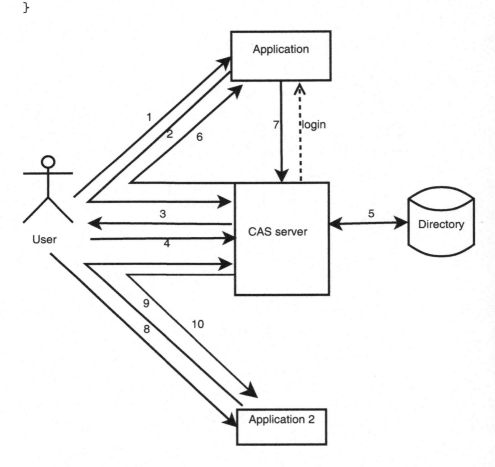

Figure 5.10. *Since the user is already known to the CAS server, the browser is redirected to the second application with a new ticket*

In practice, this script will be executed twice. The first time, it redirects the browser to the CAS server. Once the CAS server responds, it will provide a link with a ticket, and the CAS client will be able to retrieve the account.

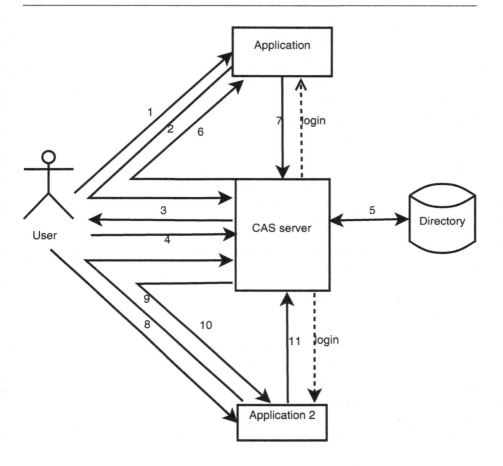

Figure 5.11. *The second application retrieves the login from the CAS server*

It is also important to manage the logout process by telling the CAS server that it should disconnect the user. A full script is given below. We begin by disabling the session cookie, by setting it to have expired:

```
// Deactivate the session cookie
if (isset ( $_COOKIE [session_name ()] )) {
    setcookie ( session_name (), '', time () -
        42000, '/' );
}
```

We then send a logout request to the server (*logout* command).

```
phpCAS::client ( CAS_VERSION_2_0 , $this ->
    CAS_address , $this ->CAS_port , $this ->CAS_uri );

phpCAS::logout ( $return_address );
```

We can optionally specify a return address to the CAS server. If this argument is not given, the user's browser will remain on the CAS server logout page. Otherwise, it will be redirected to the specified page, which could, for example, display a message stating that the user was successfully logged out.

Deleting the PHP session is not necessary. The current version of the CAS client takes care of this when the following commands are executed:

```
session_unset ();
session_destroy ();
```

CAS servers have many advantages: the application no longer needs to manage the login process or password storage, and never sees the user's password. CAS servers also support complex mechanisms for verifying the user's identity, if necessary using digital certificates or even smart card readers, which would usually be too difficult to integrate into classical management applications.

However, this technology has a disadvantage: all users must be known by the CAS server. If you need to provide services to persons who cannot be identified by this server (for example, if some application users are not part of the company and are not listed in its directory), this approach cannot be used. Indeed, the CAS server has a dedicated login screen: before the user logs in, there is no way of deciding whether to use the CAS server interface or the application interface.

We can, however, combine both approaches by creating a login button that leads to the CAS server, but this requires users that log in through the server to go through an extra screen.

If we wish to conserve a single approach with one single login screen, we can also combine a LDAP login with a database login. If logging in with the

LDAP directory is unsuccessful, the application can attempt to log in with the information stored in the database. This is often the simplest solution to implement for extranet-type applications.

5.1.5. *Doing more with CAS: identity federations with Shibboleth*

For large organizations or groups of organizations, the need for different CAS servers to communicate among themselves quickly arises. For example, a scientist conducting research might need to connect to a university or laboratory network while traveling. They might wish to use one of the many tools available to the community as a whole.

To respond to this need, identity federations have been created to group together the CAS servers of different organizations. This can, for example, enable a scientist to connect to the wireless network of a foreign research center using his or her own login information. If the local CAS server cannot find a match for the information provided by the researcher, it redirects the login request to the researcher's own center.

Although the CAS procedure is good enough for wireless connections, it has one limitation: only the login is given to the application. In some cases, it can be useful to gather more information about the identity of users (for example, first and last names), or even the name of their laboratory, or information about the groups to which they belong in the directory of their establishment.

The Shibboleth project [SHI 16], which builds upon CAS servers, allows additional information to be exchanged.

However, it is complex to implement and there are very few examples in PHP. It seems reasonable to expect that this technology will fulfill its promises and become more easy to implement in applications as it is gradually supported by more and more organizations.

We will see that additional information can be provided during the login process by using a token rather than a CAS server.

5.1.6. *Managing login offline using database storage*

All of the login methods that we discussed above assume that the client, i.e. the interface that manages the interactions with the application, is a browser. Browsers store a session cookie that allows them to use the same context for all requests sent by the same user.

In some situations, the web application will only be used to send information to client applications other than browsers, using technologies such as web services. The web server provides information in the form of a JSON or XML file: in both cases, the data are sent as text formatted either with tags or labels.

Cookie-based session management is more difficult in this context. This makes it tricky to identify users: if the application works fully offline, i.e. without keeping a session open, users will need to retype their username and password for each query. This an inefficient and expensive use of resources: each login test will need to be repeated every time. Moreover, it becomes difficult to disconnect the user after a period of inactivity if there are no tracking mechanisms.

However, the client application can store a value given by the server, for example after completing a login-related request. If this code is also saved by the server, it can be resent with each request and matched with the user's login.

This code should be randomly generated: by using cryptographic functions to guarantee uniqueness, it can provide a good way of verifying the client's identity.

The *account/generated code* pair can be stored by the server, for example in a database table. If it is associated with timestamps documenting the time of creation or the query, it can be used to implement a maximum connection period and a maximum allowable period between two requests, which provides userful information to resource controllers (see section 4.4). The IP address can also be saved to verify that the client has not changed between two queries, which might indicate identity theft.

To implement this mechanism, we need to create a database table to manage the process of storing and validating this code (Figure 5.12).

logintag	
Table of labels associated with logins	
◆ logintag_id	integer
● login	varchar
● tag	varchar
● login_date	timestamp
○ last_request	timestamp
○ ip_address	varchar

Figure 5.12. _Table structure for generating a code based on the login_

This table has an automatic key, _logintag_id_. It also has a column for storing the login, and another whose value is calculated and sent to the client application. Finally, the table contains datetimes: one for the time of login and one for the time of the most recent query. The first of these values (_login_date_) can be used to define a maximum duration for work sessions, independently of which operations are performed. The second value, _last_request_, can be used to manage the maximum inactivity period. This value is updated with each query, and if the time elapsed since the most recent query becomes too large, the session is closed.

The last field stores the client's IP address. Any change in this value during a work session might indicate session hijacking. In such a case, it is a good idea to disconnect the user and ask him/her to repeat the login process.

We will now present each of the functions that we will be needed for this. The first generates a random code. We will begin by reusing the random code-generating function encountered earlier (see section 5.1.1).

```
function getRandomCode($length=64) {
    return bin2hex( openssl_random_pseudo_bytes(
        $length));
}
```

This function generates a code of 128 characters (64 hexadecimal characters).

The next function manages the connection. The first time, the application provides the user's login and password, and returns the code that will be used for the subsequent steps:

```
function loginSet($login, $password) {
    /*
     * Check the validity of the login/password
       pair
     */
    if (loginVerify($login, $password) == 1) {
        /*
         * connect to the database
         */
        $dsn = 'pgsql:dbname=database;host
            =127.0.0.1';
        $user = 'dbuser';
        $password = 'dbpass';

        try {
            $dbh = new PDO($dsn, $user, $password);
        } catch (PDOException $e) {
            echo 'Connection failed: ' . $e->
                getMessage();
        }
        /*
         * get the tag that will be sent to the
           client application
         */
        $tag = getRandomCode();
        /*
         * prepare query to insert a new record
         * into the database
         */
        $currentDate = date ("Y-m-d H:i:s");
        $sql = "insert into logintag (login, tag,
            login_date, last_request, ip_address)
                      values (:login, :tag, :
                          currentDate, :currentDate,
```

```
                            :ip)";
        $data = array("login"=>$login,
                "tag"=>$tag,
                "currentDate"=>$currentDate,
                "ip"=>getClientIPAddress());
        $stmt = $dbh->prepare($sql);
        $stmt->execute($data);
        return $tag;
        }
    }
}
```

The *loginVerify()* function is not implemented here and needs to be written specifically for the application.

This function not only generates the code and returns it, but also creates a record in the database to store it.

We used a dedicated function to find the client's IP address, which we discussed earlier (see section 4.2.2).

One more function still needs to be written: the function that fetches the login account given the code.

We begin by defining the maximum duration between two queries and the maximum duration for the work session:

```
function getLoginFromTag($tag) {
    /*
     * maximum duration parameters, in seconds
     */
    $maxSessionDuration = 43200; // 12 hours
    $maxDurationBetweenRequest = 3600; // 1 hour
```

We then establish the database connection and search for a record that matches the code:

```
    if (strlen($tag) > 0) {
        /*
         * connect to the database
```

```
*/
$dsn = 'pgsql:dbname=database;host
    =127.0.0.1';
$user = 'dbuser';
$password = 'dbpass';

try {
    $dbh = new PDO($dsn, $user, $password);
} catch (PDOException $e) {
    echo 'Connection failed: ' . $e->
        getMessage();
}
/*
 * Prepare the query
 */
$sql = "select * from logintag
     where tag = ?
     order by login_date desc";
$stmt = $dbh->prepare($sql);
$stmt->bindParam(1, $tag);
if ($stmt->execute() {
  $row = $stmt->fetch();
```

The query is returned in decreasing order of connection date, and only the first record is selected. This eliminates the risk of collision, i.e., the possibility that the same code was generated twice. Given the cryptographic nature of the process, this is unlikely, but by taking this precaution it becomes reasonable to expect that it will never happen.

We now also check that the IP address hasn't changed, using the function we defined before:

```
$testOk = true;
/*
 * Check the IP address
 */
if (getClientIPAddress() == $row["
    ip_address"]) {
```

and we also verify that the total duration of the session and the period between two sessions do not exceed the chosen thresholds:

```
/*
 * Check durations
 */
$currentDate = date()->getDatestamp();
$lastRequest = date_create_from_format
    ("Y-m-d H:i:s", $row["last_request
    "])->getDatestamp() ;
$interval = $currentDate -
    $lastRequest;
if ($interval <=
    $maxDurationBetweenRequest) {
    $loginDate =
        date_create_from_format ("Y-m-d
        H:i:s", $row["login_date"])->
        getDatestamp() ;
    $interval = $currentDate -
        $loginDate;
    if ($interval >
        $maxDurationBetweenRequest)
        $testOk = false;
} else
    $testOk = false;
} else
    $testOk = false;
if ($testOk == true) {
```

If all tests are successfully passed, the record is updated with the current time of the query being processed:

```
/*
 * Update the time of the most recent
    request
 */
$sql = "update logintag set
    last_request = ?
        where logintag_id = ?";
```

```
$stup = $dbh->prepare($sql);
$stup->bindParam(1, date ("Y-m-d H:i:
    s"));
$stup->bindParam(2,$row["logintag_id
    "]);
$stup->execute();
/*
 * return login
 */
```

Finally, we return the login value:

```
return $row["login"];
    }
  }
}
```

If this value is not null, then the code provided was correct, and the login is the same as the one provided by the user. The application can then check which permissions are associated with the account and continue to process the request.

The advantage of using this procedure is that connections can be separated from each other. The same user can log in from multiple different devices or software programs, for example both a Java program and a classical web application, without the risk of mixing up information: the generated *tag* value is random and unique.

This mechanism can be extended to store session variables, if necessary, by adding an additional column in the table.

5.1.7. *Managing the login process using a token encrypted with asymmetric keys*

The above method is based on storing a token matching the user's login in the database.

It has two disadvantages. Firstly, a storage table must be available, and a query must be executed for each operation to retrieve the login account. The second issue is slightly more serious. With this procedure, the application that generated the token is the only one that can use it. The login cannot therefore be handed over to a dedicated program unless the database is shared.

The method that we will examine now sends an encrypted file to the user containing the login and expiration date, rather than just a token whose value has no special significance.

The simplest way of guaranteeing the origin of the token is to use asymmetric encryption.

As we saw earlier, the principle of asymmetric encryption is based on two keys. Any information encrypted with one can only be decrypted with the other. In practice, the server holds one of these: the private key. The other key is distributed to any customers that need it, if necessary by wrapping it in a certificate that guarantees its origin.

Any message encrypted with the private key can be decrypted with the public key. If the server encrypts the token with its private key, it can only be decrypted with the server's public key, which guarantees the origin of the token.

This mechanism allows us to entrust the login to a third-party server: the application server simply requires the public key of the login server to decrypt the token and retrieve the login. This approach also has the advantage of not requiring a token to be stored by the login server (we could have suggested associating a random token with each login), which makes the application easier to code. Finally, application web servers already have certificates (private and signed public keys) to support HTTPS-mode connections.

The sequence diagram below explains how this works (Figure 5.14).

It works as follows:

– the user logs in for the first time with the server by entering their login and password;

– the server checks this information, then creates a file containing the login and expiration date;

– it encrypts this file with its private key, then encodes it in base 64 to send it as text;

Token containing the login,   {"login":"eric.quinton"}
in JSON format

private key

Token encrypted and
based64 encoded   cFsuv+129Gmr1ivi3f0t
so it can be sent as a text

public key

Token decoded   {"login":"eric.quinton"}
and decrypted

Figure 5.13. *Asymmetric encryption of a token*

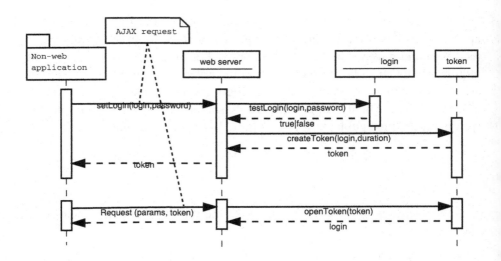

Figure 5.14. *General diagram for the asymmetric encryption of a token*

– the encrypted file (the token) is sent to the user (the client application);

– when users need to interact with the server, they add the token to their request;

– when the server receives a request, it decodes then decrypts the token using its public key. It can then check the expiration date and retrieve the login.

– the rest can be done as usual: the server can use this login as if the user had logged in conventionally.

We will now see how this mechanism can be implemented.

First, we initialize a class by indicating the location of the private key and the public key (the default parameters can be modified at instantiation):

```
class Token {
    private $privateKey = "/etc/ssl/private/ssl-
        cert-snakeoil.key";
    private $pubKey = "/etc/ssl/certs/ssl-cert-
        snakeoil.pem";
    private $validityDuration = 86400;

    function __construct($privateKey = "", $pubKey
        = "") {
        if (strlen ( $privateKey ) > 0)
            $this->privateKey = $privateKey;
        if (strlen ( $pubKey ) > 0)
            $this->pubKey = $pubKey;
    }
```

The *$validityDuration* stores the default lifetime of a token, which here is equal to one day (in seconds).

We can create the token as follows. The function accepts two input parameters: the login and the duration of validity.

```
function createToken ($login, $validityDuration
    = -1) {
    $tokenOk = false;
    if (strlen ( $login ) > 0) {
```

The expiration date of the token is calculated:

```
if ( is_numeric ( $validityDuration )) {
   $timestamp = time ();
   $validityDuration > - 1 ? $expire =
      $timestamp + $validityDuration :
      $expire = $timestamp + $this ->
      validityDuration;
```

Then an array is created containing various values, and converted into a JSON string:

```
$data = array (
       "login" => $login ,
       "timestamp" => $timestamp ,
       "expire" => $expire
);
/*
 * create json file
 */
$tokenJSON = json_encode ( $data );
```

The JSON string is encrypted with the private key. The token thus obtained is encoded in *base 64*[2], then saved in another JSON variable so that it can finally be sent to the browser or client application:

```
$key = $this ->getKey ( "priv" );
if (openssl_private_encrypt (
   $tokenJSON , $crypted , $key )) {
   /*
    * prepare file with base64
      encoding
    */
   $dataToken = array (
          "token" => base64_encode (
             $crypted ),
```

---

2 This format allows us to transform a binary file into text so that it can be sent using web protocols.

```
            "expire" => $expire,
            "timestamp" => $data ["
                timestamp"]
        );
        $tokenOk = true;
        $token = json_encode ( $dataToken )
            ;
```

Finally, the function ends with an exception handler to manage any potential errors:

```
        } else
            throw new Exception ( "
                Encryption_token_not_realized" )
                ;
        } else
            throw new Exception ( "validity
                duration not numeric : " .
                $validityDuration );
    } else
        throw new Exception ( "login_empty" );
    return $token;
}
```

The token can be read as follows. The function accepts a token either in the form of a variable or an array.

```
function openToken($token) {
    if (! is_array ( $token ))
        $token = array (
                "token" => $token
        );
    /*
     * decrypt token
     */
```

The token is decoded, then decrypted with the public key:

```
    if (strlen ( $token ["token"] ) > 0) {
        $key = $this->getKey ( "pub" );
```

```
if (openssl_public_decrypt (
    base64_decode ( $token ["token"] ),
    $decrypted, $key )) {
    $data = json_decode ( $decrypted, true
        );
```

Once decrypted, the program checks that the token has not expired by comparing the transmitted date with the current date, and populates the *$login* variable, which is returned:

```
/*
 * Verification of token content
 */
if (strlen ( $data ["login"] ) > 0 &&
    strlen ( $data ["expire"] ) > 0) {
    $now = time ();
    /*
     * test expire date
     */
    if ($data ["expire"] > $now) {
        $login = $data ["login"];
```

Similarly to the function for generating the token, it ends by declaring exceptions for unexpected events:

```
} else
    throw new Exception ( '
        token_expired' );
} else
    throw new Exception ( "
        parameter_into_token_absent" );
} else
    throw new Exception ( "
        token_cannot_be_decrypted" );
} else
    throw new Exception ( "token_empty" );
return $login;
}
```

We need one last function to read the private or public keys:

```
private function getKey($type = "priv") {
    $contents = "";
    if ($type == "priv" || $type == "pub") {
        $type == "priv" ? $filename = $this->
            privateKey : $filename = $this->pubKey
            ;
        if (file_exists ( $filename )) {
            $handle = fopen ( $filename, "r" );
            if (! $handle == false) {
                $contents = fread ( $handle,
                    filesize ( $filename ) );
                if ($contents == false)
                    throw new Exception ( "key " .
                        $filename . " is empty" );
                fclose ( $handle );
            } else
                throw new Exception ( $filename . "
                    could not be open" );
        } else
            throw new Exception ( "key " .
                $filename . " not found" );
    } else
        throw new Exception ( "open key : type
            not specified" );
    return $contents;
    }
}
```

This function is entirely straightforward. It also includes an error handler so that it is compatible with the rest of the class.

We will now see how everything can be implemented using a short script that creates the token, decrypts it, then retrieves the login that it contains.

We begin by loading the file containing the class, and create a pseudo-function to simulate the login:

```
include_once 'token.class.php';

function verifyLogin($login, $password) {
   return true;
}
```

Prepare a login input form:

```
$tokenClass = new Token ();
if (! isset ( $_GET ["token"] ) && ! isset ( $_GET
   ["login"] )) {
   /*
    * 1st step
    * Login input form
    */
   echo '<html><form method="get" action="
      createToken.php">';
   echo 'login : <input name="login"><br>';
   echo 'password : <input type="password" name="
      password"><br>';
   echo '<input type="submit"></form></html>';
```

The *login* variable will be sent to the application: we can now generate the token and prepare a form to submit it to the server.

```
} else {
   if (isset ( $_GET ["login"] )) {
      /*
       * 2st step
       * generate the token and send it to the
         browser
       */
      if (verifyLogin ( $_GET ["login"], $_GET ["
         password"] )) {

         try {
            /*
             * create the token valid for one hour
             */
```

```
        $token = $tokenClass ->createToken (
          $_GET ["login"], 3600 );
        echo $token ."<br>";
        /*
         * Prepare the test form to be
           submitted
         */
        $content = json_decode ( $token , true
          );
        echo '<html ><form method =" get " action
          =" createToken . php">';
        echo '<input name =" token " value ="' .
          $content ["token"] . '"><br>';
        echo '<input type =" submit "></form ></
          html >';
    } catch ( Exception $e ) {
      echo $e ->getMessage ();
    }
  }
```

This form displays the encrypted token, encoded in base64. The final step is to validate this token, i.e., decrypt it and display the corresponding login:

```
} else {
  /*
   * 3rd step
   * Process the token to read its content
   */
  try {
    $login = $tokenClass ->openToken ( $_GET
      ["token"] );
    echo "login : " . $login;
  } catch ( Exception $e ) {
    echo $e ->getMessage ();
  }
}
}
```

This method has many advantages. The server does not need to save the login/key pair, as the token contains the identifier. Even if the encrypted file is decrypted (it can be decrypted with the public key), it does not contain any confidential information. If it is modified, it cannot be re-encrypted, since the server has the only copy of the private key required to do so.

The login process can also be delegated to another server or application: the fact that the public key is used to decrypt the token guarantees its origin.

Finally, the expiration date is associated with the login: it is very easy to check that the submitted account is valid.

The method that we considered earlier has other advantages: in particular, it allows any token to be immediately invalidated, which is not possible with this procedure. Indeed, no records of the generated token are kept, so it remains valid until it expires.

These two techniques are broadly equivalent in terms of security, at least on the surface, but they respond to slightly different objectives. You are free to decide which is the most suitable for your own application.

5.1.8. *Creating tokens with the JWT protocol*

The token that we created earlier allows the server to verify the identity of the party submitting a request. Implementing this mechanism only requires a few dozen lines, including error handling.

When the token was sent to the client, we wrapped it in a JSON file that can also carry other information (such as the username). However, this is not a very satisfactory approach: although the token itself is self-sufficient for the login, if other associated information is sent with it, the client needs to know how it was generated and transmitted in order to interpret it. For private or limited-scope applications, this is not a problem, but if the service is intended to be used by a wide variety of client applications, it might be worth considering a standardized protocol.

Json Web Tokens (JWT) [JWT 16]) are a standardized protocol for managing tokens.

The token has three parts. The header describes the encryption method used to sign it. The body contains the transmitted information, which in our case is the login and expiration date, and the final part contains the signature.

The token is divided into its three parts as follows:

`xxxx.yyyy.zzzz`

Each part is encoded in base64 to guarantee that it is transferred in web mode, and is separated from the other parts by a period.

xxxx is the header. Its content is formatted in JSON, and only includes the name of the encryption method. The following shows the example of asymmetric encryption based on public/private keys:

```
{
    "alg": "RS256",
    "typ": "JWT"
}
```

yyyy contains the useful content of the token, i.e., the information to be transmitted.

The protocol defines so-called private variables with three-letter names to limit the volume of transmitted information. The most common variables are summarized in Table 5.1.

Code	Full name	Description
iss	Issuer	Name of the party issuing the token
sub	Subject	Primary usage
aud	Audience	Describes the intended recipient of the token
exo	Expiration time	Expiration date/time (formatted as a timestamp)
nbf	Not before	Indicates the date/time when the token first becomes valid
iat	Issued at	Date/time at which the token was generated
jti	JWT ID	Unique token identifier

Table 5.1. *Most common variable names used by the JWT protocol*

All of these values are optional.

Custom values can also be added. Table 5.2 summarizes the values that are relevant to our chosen usage example:

Code	Description
uid	*userId*, Login account
cn	*Common name*, First and last names of the individual
sn	*Surname*, Last name
gvn	*givenName*, First name

Table 5.2. *Examples of possible additional variables*

These are the attributes that are typically used by LDAP directories.

The following gives an example of the content of a token:

```
{
    "exp":"12345678",
    "uid":"eric.quinton",
    "cn":"Eric Quinton",
    "sn":"Quinton",
    "gvn":"Eric"
}
```

The first two values are required by the server to verify the token and retrieve the login. The others can be used by client applications to display text if necessary (*Welcome, Eric Quinton*, for example).

zzzz contains the result of the encrypting the first two parts, *xxxx.yyyy*, which is used as the signature.

The advantage of this approach is that each part can be considered independently of the other parts, depending on what we want to do with them. Thus, if a client application wants to access the transmitted data, it simply needs to decrypt *yyyy* and retrieve the variables that it contains.

Similarly, if the server only accepts a single protocol, it does not need to decode the first part. It can simply check the signature and decrypt the body to retrieve the login.

There are many implementations of this mechanism in PHP. One of the most comprehensive was developed by Luís Otávio Cobucci Oblonczyk [COB 16].

5.1.9. *Using the OAuth protocol to generate tokens*

Sometimes, applications need to access information that belongs to the user but is held by another website. For example (this example is presented on the project website), suppose Alice wishes to connected to an application (APP-1) for printing photos. Her photos are hosted on another platform (APP-2). The objective is for Alice to be able to log into APP-2 and give APP-1 the right to retrieve the photos without Alice having to re-upload them herself.

The OAuth [OAU 16] protocol can be used to meet this need. It is very similar to the CAS login mechanism we discussed earlier.

The exchange unfolds as follows:

– APP-1 registers with APP-2 beforehand, and obtains an account and password;

– Alice logs into APP-1, and states that her photos are hosted by APP-2

– APP-1 redirects Alice to APP-2. She logs in, and authorizes APP-1 to retrieve the photos;

– APP-2 redirects Alice to APP-1, providing a token that temporarily authorizes access;

– APP-1 uses this temporary authorization to retrieve the photos, and then print them.

The OAuth protocol provides various integrated mechanisms for protecting this exchange. APP-1 needs its own token. The authorization that it obtains is wrapped in a single-use token with an expiration date. Finally, a hash is appended to prevent the information from being modified.

There are two versions of this protocol. Version 2.0 was developed to make it easier to implement in client applications, particularly those running on modern devices (tablets, smartphones, etc.). However, it is not compatible with version 1.0.

Several large companies, such as Amazon, Instagram, Google just to name a few, support logging in using this mechanism. The easiest way of implementing it into an application is to refer to the documentation provided by these companies, in particular to know how to manage error codes and other implementation details, depending on the language you are using (PHP, JavaScript, or other).

5.2. Managing permissions

The final step in securing an application is proper permissions management.

Before beginning to program, it is important to define the granularity of these permissions, i.e., the way that they are applied. Should we manage global permissions separately for each big module (application administration, reference table management, customer file management), or by action type (reading, modifying, deleting). Or should we combine them?

The second question relates to the way that user accounts are managed. Should permissions be assigned individually, or based on existing groups (for example those in the company directory), or by creating specific groups within the application?

5.2.1. *What should we protect?*

Typically, several big modules can be identified within an application: permissions management, parameter and reference table management, a module for monitoring customer files (or multiple for different types of customer file). The conventional operations performed on these modules are reading, inserting, updating, and deleting information.

To make it easier to define the permissions that need to be assigned, it can be useful to begin by creating a summary Table 5.3:

The columns of this table show the possible actions, ordered increasingly by level, and the rows give the modules of the application.

The second step is to define the global permissions that will be managed by the application. Generic permissions such as *read* for viewing information, *manage* for editing information, *param* for managing reference tables, and *admin* for assigning permissions are commonly used. They can also differ between modules to differentiate the way that permissions are managed throughout the application.

Module or function	Read	Insert	Update	Delete
User administration				
Reference tables				
Customer file type 1				
Customer file type 2				

Table 5.3. *Summary table of permissions to be assigned*

It's helpful to populate the table shown above with the names of these permissions.

Consider the following example. In our software application, any user can view the reference tables, and any user with access to the user administration module has full access. However, deleting a reference requires special permissions, and so does adding or deleting the information from a *type-2 customer file*.

Table 5.4 shows a usage example.

Family	Read	Insert	Update	Delete
User administration	admin	admin	admin	admin
Reference tables	read, manageRef, adminRef	manageRef, adminRef	manageRef, adminRef	adminRef
Customer file type 1	read, updateFile1, adminFile1	adminFile1	updateFile1, adminFile1	adminFile1
Customer file type 2	read, manageFile2	manageFile2	manageFile2	manageFile2

Table 5.4. *Example of populated permissions summary table*

Some operations can be performed by several different permissions, which is realistic: the administrator of a customer file can also view it.

The permissions thus defined will be tested to determine whether access to each function of the application should be granted or blocked. To do this, we need to individualize each action that requires a permission. The simplest way is to create one page or link for each action:

– *index.php?module=refDisplay* to display a reference table,

– *index.php?module=refAdd* to add a new entry,

– *index.php?module=refUpdate* to update an existing entry,

– *index.php?module=refDelete* to delete an entry.

In practice, we also need to display a form for updating entries, which requires us to introduce the following link before calling the update or delete functions:

– *index.php?module=refChange*

which uses the same permissions as the update function. Updating an entry and creating an entry is essentially the same thing, except that in the latter case the key of the entry is not known, which leads to execute an *insert* command rather than an *update* command in the database[3].

If we wish to use several different links, we either need a mechanism for rewriting the target address of the form or separate forms for each action.

In the following example, the delete and update buttons are located in different forms:

```
<div class="inputForm">
<fieldset>
<legend>Recurrence table</legend>
<div>

<form method="post" action="index.php?module=
    recurrenceWrite">
```

---

3 Simultaneously managing both insert and update commands with a single form is relatively straightforward. We can for example adopt the convention that all new records have identifier 0. Then simply testing this value allows us to distinguish between the two cases.

```
<input type="hidden" name="recurrence_id" value
    ="1">

<dl>
<dt>Content<span class="red">*</span> :</dt>
<dd><input class="comment" id="recurrence_label"
    name="recurrence_label" value="Continuous"
    required> </dd>
</dl>
<dl>
<div class="buttonForm">
<input class="submit" type="submit" value="Save">
</div>
</form>

<div class="buttonForm">
<form action="index.php" method="post" onSubmit='
    return confirmDeletion("Are you sure you want
    to delete?")'>
<input type="hidden" name="recurrence_id" value
    ="1">
<input type="hidden" name="module" value="
    recurrenceDelete">
<input class="submit" type="submit" value="Delete
    ">

</form>
</div>
</div>
</fieldset>
</div>
<span class="red">*</span><span class="
    bottommessage">Required field</span>
</div>
```

This page contains two forms, even though visually the user only sees one. The first calls the *recurrenceWrite* module, the second calls the *recurrenceDelete* module.

Here, the input grid is displayed using description lists (*<dl>* tags).

The record is only deleted subject to the condition that the user has the appropriate permissions, which the application will verify when it receives the information submitted by the browser. Each module simply needs to test which permissions are required to either authorize or block the execution of the code.

Another alternative is to use a single form with JavaScript code to switch between operations.

The following JavaScript code manages the action that will be executed:

```
$(document).ready(
   function() {
   $('.button-delete').keypress(function() {
      if (confirm("Are you sure that you want to
          delete?") == true) {
         $(this.form).find("input[name='action']")
            .val("Delete");
         $(this.form).submit();
      } else
         return false;
   });
   $( ".button-delete" ).click(function() {
      if (confirm("Are you sure that you want to
          delete?") == true) {
         $(this.form).find("input[name='action']")
            .val("Delete");
         $(this.form).submit();
      } else {
         return false;
      }
   });
)};
```

This code changes the value of the *action* field in the form when the button with the *button-delete* class is pressed (either by clicking or using the keyboard).

The code for the form becomes the following:

```
<input type="hidden" name="moduleBase" value="app
   ">
<input type="hidden" name="action" value="Write">
(...)
<input type="submit" value="Confirm">
<input type="submit class="button-delete" value="
   Delete">
```

We now need to deduce which module should be executed when the form is received by the server:

```
<?php
if (isset ( $_REQUEST ["moduleBase"] ) && isset (
   $_REQUEST ["action"] ))
      $_REQUEST ["module"] = $_REQUEST ["moduleBase"]
         . $_REQUEST ["action"];
?>
```

The *module* value is generated from two pieces of information contained in the form, namely *moduleBase* and *action*.

5.2.2. *Managing user permissions with LDAP directory groups*

Now that we know how to protect access to our modules, we will discuss how to manage the process of assigning permissions.

There are several possible scenarios.

In a company, it might be the case that some information is visible to every employee. If the login process is based on a LDAP directory or a CAS server, the corresponding permissions simply need to be assigned when the login process finishes. The advantage of this approach is that it avoids having to manually authorize every user to access an application that is intended to be accessible to the whole company.

Access can alternatively be restricted to specific groups declared in the LDAP directory. Again, the objective is to trust the company directory. This ensures that application access is always consistent with changes in personnel.

We can check whether a user belongs to a directory group as follows.

We begin by connecting to the LDAP directory (the variables are assumed to have been populated earlier):

```
$idldap = @ldap_connect($LDAP_address,$LDAP_port)
  ;
  if ($idldap > 0) {
        if ($LDAP_v3 == 1) {
            ldap_set_option($idldap,
                LDAP_OPT_PROTOCOL_VERSION, 3);
        }
        if ($LDAP_tls == 1)
        {
            ldap_start_tls($idldap);
        }
```

We now declare the properties that we are interested in. In this case, we retrieve the last name (*sn* attribute) and first name (*givenName* attribute) of the individual, as well as the attributes of a Microsoft *Active Directory*, namely the service name (*departmentNumber*) and entity to which the individual was assigned (*supannAssignedEntity*). We will deduce permissions from the last of these attributes.

```
$attribute = array (
    "sn",
    "givenName",
    "departmentNumber",
    "supannAssignedEntity"
);
```

The login is stored in the session variable *$_SESSION ["login"]*. We prepare the query filter and launch the search:

```
$basedn="ou=people,dc=company,dc=com";
$filter= "(uid=" . $_SESSION ["login"] . ")
    ";
```

```
$sr = ldap_search($idldap,$basedn,$filter,
    $attribute);
$data = ldap_get_entries($idldap, $sr);
```

The *$data* array contains all of the attributes associated with the user. We now simply need to find the values contained in the *supannAssignedEntity* attribute and compare them with the authorized groups to determine whether the user has the correct permissions (here, *manage*):

```
if ($data ["count"] > 0) {
    $loginGroups = array_flip($data [0] ["
        supannassignedentity"]);

    $groups = array("department1", "
        department2");
    /*
     * Assign the manage permission if part
        of an authorized group
     */
    foreach ($groups as $key=>$value)
        if (isset($loginGroups [$value ["
            group_name"]]))
            $_SESSION["rights"]["manage"] = 1;
    }
  }
}
```

This is a useful mechanism, but it can prove insufficient of the groups defined in the LDAP directory that do not match the project requirements. If so, we need to resort to user management directly within the application.

5.2.3. *Managing user permissions based on groups defined in the application*

In the 2000s, the *phpgacl* project [PHP 06] was one of the richest and most comprehensive tools for managing permissions. Unfortunately, it has not been maintained since 2006, and its permissions management interface has since become obsolete, and, importantly, is susceptible to several security vulnerabilities.

However, the conceptual approach of the project remains interesting. It used a list of permissions, which can be different for each application, as well as a hierarchy-based system for user groups. It allowed a unique database to be created containing the permissions granted to users for applications.

The following kind of hierarchy is easy to implement (Figure 5.15):

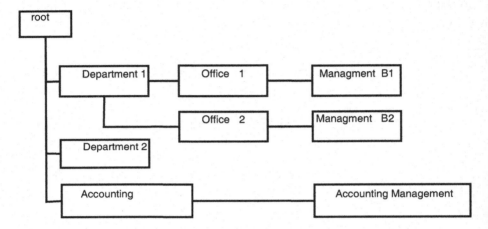

Figure 5.15. *User group hierarchy tree*

This has several useful features. First, we can mix organizational groups (departments, offices, etc.) with thematic and functional groups. Also, each user placed in a group also becomes a member of all parent groups, to the left. Therefore, if viewing permissions are granted to *Department 1*, the users in *Office 1* and *Management O2* are also granted the same permissions.

Users can belong to multiple groups. The same account can be listed under *Office 1* and *Accounting*, endowing it with the permissions awarded to each of these groups (and their predecessors in the hierarchy).

To grant all of these permissions within the application, we need two additional tables. The first allows us to specify which accounts are associated with which groups.

login	Office 1	Office 2	Accounting	Accounting management
john.smith		X		
freddy.francis	X		X	
james.jackson	X		X	
martha.miller		X		

Table 5.5. *Simplified table of the accounts associated with each group*

The second table lists the permissions granted to each group:

Group	View	ManageFile	ManageRef	Admin
root (company)	X			
Office 1		X		
Office 2		X		
Accounting			X	
Accounting management				X

Table 5.6. *Summary table of permissions to be assigned*

With the above distribution of permissions, all registered users have viewing permissions, and only accounts belonging to the *Accounting Management* group are administrators.

We will now discuss how to implement this approach. There are naturally several possible ways of doing so, such as to declare these permissions in an XML file or a database. We will consider the latter option in more detail.

Figure 5.16 shows one possible way of structuring our permissions database.

The *login* table contains a list of the accounts registered to the application. These accounts are assigned to one or multiple groups (*group* table). Groups can themselves belong to other groups: this allows permissions to be recursively defined, i.e. accounts can inherit the permissions of lower level groups.

Access Control Objects (*aco* table), and the permissions managed by each application, are specified separately for each software (*software* table). This approach allows us to define a single permissions database for a range of different programs or modules if we so desire.

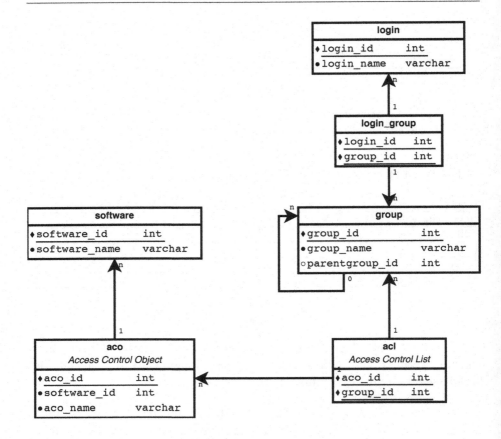

Figure 5.16. *Organizational model for the database*

Finally, the last table, the *acl* table (*Access Control List*), contains the links between permissions and login groups.

The following algorithm finds the permissions of a given account (Figure 5.17):

The principle of this process is relatively simple, but it can be expensive to execute. It requires multiple database queries, and the manager class of the mechanism can include several hundred lines of code. In practice, we should avoid executing it more than once. We can run it immediately after the user logs in and then store the array of permissions as a session variable. The code below gives an example (without giving the full code for extracting permissions, which would be too cumbersome):

```
$rights = new Rights();
$_SESSION["rights"] = $rights->getList( $_SESSION
    ["login"] );
```

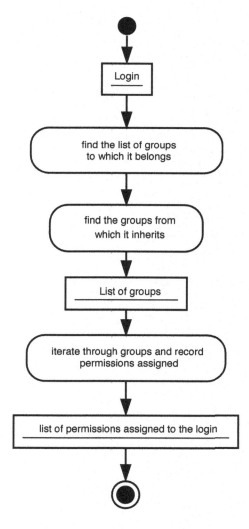

Figure 5.17. *Algorithm for determining the permissions of an account*

The simplest approach is to store these permissions in an array, as follows:

```
$_SESSION["rights"]=array("right1"=>1, "right2
    "=>1);
```

In the application code, we check this array to determine whether the user has the required permissions:

```
if ($_SESSION["rights"]["right1"] == 1)
    echo "right ok";
```

5.3. In summary

Access control must be applied to every page and module of the application. Each operation (viewing, updating, deleting, etc.) must be handled separately.

Users should ideally log in through a CAS server that is connected to the company directory. By default, LDAP queries are preferable to using a database to store users. If a database is used, precautions must be taken to protect the list of users: encryption, password salting, recovery procedures based on single-usage links, etc.

User access permissions are managed by groups, which can be hierarchically defined (groups can belong to other groups). Access permissions are defined per module and per operation (insertion, update, etc.) and assigned to these groups.

Using the MVC Model to Structure the Application

6.1. Why does the application structure matter?

Securing an application requires us to implement a large number of checks and components, each with its own role. Each check or component relates to a different aspect of the application: verifying the data sent to the server, logging and managing permissions, protecting the database, encoding the data sent to the browser and encrypting the connection, etc.

Twenty years ago, security only required two or three functions that were relatively easy to copy from one page to another. Today, the sheer complexity of the mechanisms that must be implemented renders this approach obsolete: it is essential to group together the protective functions in the relevant parts of the application.

Similarly, the code was relatively simple in early software. Computers generally had equivalent screen sizes, with slow processing power, and the speed of Internet connections was limited (downloading pages larger than 200 KB created issues). Programmers limited their scripts to only what was strictly necessary, and object-oriented programming was criticized due to the loss of performance associated with it.

Today, every modern PHP application has several thousands of lines of code, distributed over increasingly complex file systems. The "page by page" approach is no longer feasible: the only solution is to develop a high-level architecture that allows a global overview of the application structure and operation.

Several approaches have been proposed for organizing the code of such applications. The most popular is the MVC model, which has been further developed into a number of variants to meet special approaches or needs.

6.2. What is the MVC model?

The MVC model or pattern (model, view, controller) is a development structure that gives a description of three different types of behavior within the application.

The *model* layer implements all of the application logic, i.e. the sequences of operations that the software must perform to fulfill its purpose. The *view* layer displays all of the outputs generated by the application. In most cases, these outputs are displayed as webpages sent to the browser, but they can also take the form of PDF documents, JSON or XML-formatted data, etc. Finally, the *controller* orchestrates the application: it is responsible for organizing navigation throughout the application and managing calls to the processing modules.

The browser sends a request to the application. The controller intercepts this request. Before executing the requested module (the request), the controller checks that the user has the necessary permissions.

Once these checks have been performed, the module is executed. It might need to retrieve information from the database: the module can either directly query the database or use a class acting as an interface. These two blocks, the module and the database access, make up the *model* in the MVC pattern.

During execution, the module sends information to the view, which is responsible for displaying it. Once the module has finished execution, it hands control back to the controller. Depending on the application logic, the controller might then execute another module. This is usually the case for update operations: once the information has been recorded in the database, the controller will typically either ask for the list to be displayed, or for the processed information to be shown in more detail. Once all operations have been completed, the controller will ask the view to begin displaying (or send information to the browser).

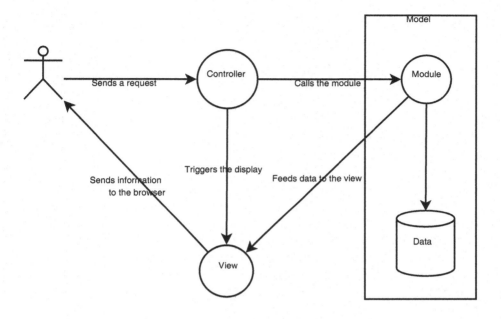

Figure 6.1. *Diagram of the MVC model*

6.2.1. *Model*

The model contains the application logic. It is often composed of two separate parts: the first manages exchanges with the database and the second contains application-specific code.

A number of security measures are implemented at this level. The submodel responsible for sending queries to the tables must implement all measures required to protect the database, such as checks to prevent SQL code injection (see section 4.2.1). In most cases, specific classes are used, sometimes known as Object Relational Mappings (ORMs) [WIK 16b], which transform the database structure (the tables) into classes that are manipulated directly by the application. These ORMs generally incorporate conventional security checks, such as measures to protect against SQL injection.

The code modules on the other hand are responsible for everything that happens before or after the database queries, such as transcoding keys as discussed earlier (see section 4.2.4).

This model feeds information to the view, using assignment commands such as:

```
$view ->set ($data , 'variableName ');
```

It does not modify the display itself: it only sends information. The view is then responsible for organizing this information into the expected format (webpage, JSON or XML file, etc.).

6.2.2. View

In the MVC model, the view is the part of the application that is sent to the user. This is usually an interface for viewing or entering information. In a web application, the view consists of the HTML pages with all of its components: the HTML code, of course, but also the stylesheets determining how this information is represented, and the JavaScript code that makes the webpages dynamic and allows calculations to be performed directly in the user's browser.

Often, webpages are generated using *template* engines. These engines add special code to the HTML code of each page to integrate the data sent by the model. Smarty [SMA 16] is one example, providing a class that generates webpages in real time, depending on the transmitted data. In this example, the view uses Smarty to generate the code sent to the browser.

Applications rarely only send webpages. AJAX requests, which allow information to be dynamically retrieved from the server without reloading the entire page, are based on the transfer of files formatted in JSON. The CSV format is often used to export data to a spreadsheet. Before sending files to the browser, we must prepare a special HTML header stating the MIME type[1].

Although the view is thought of as a single component in the MVC model, in practice there are several types of view, dedicated to sending different formats. Figure 6.2 shows an example of a view class hierarchy.

---

1 The MIME type (*Internet Media Type*) is a standard [WIK 16c] that allows us to specify the format of information to the browser. The browser can then choose the appropriate way of handling this information. For example, a file with MIME type *text/csv* can be downloaded or opened with spreadsheet software, and a PDF file will be sent with the *application/PDF* MIME type, so that it can be opened with a PDF reader.

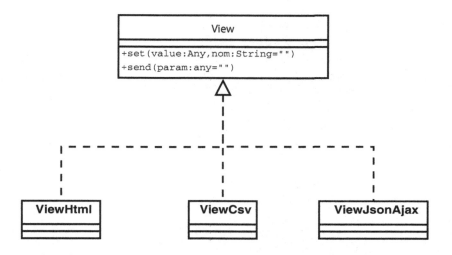

Figure 6.2. *View hierarchy*

In Figure 6.2, three classes were defined, each inheriting from an initial class that is never directly instantiated. The following shows an example implementation. The main class, View, has three functions, one of which is dedicated to security:

```
class View {
   /**
    * Data to be sent (non-html case)
    * @var array
    */
   protected $data = array ();

   /**
    * Assign a value
    * @param unknown $value
    * @param string $variable
    */
   function set($value, $variable = "") {
      $this->data = $value;
   }
   /**
```

```
 * Begin displaying
 * @param string $param
 */
function send($param = "") {
}
/**
 * Recursive html encoding function
 * for variables
 *
 * @param string|array $data
 * @return string
 */
function encodehtml($data) {
    if (is_array ( $data )) {
        foreach ( $data as $key => $value ) {
            $data [$key] = $this ->encodehtml (
                $value );
        }
    } else {
        $data = htmlspecialchars ( $data );
    }
    return $data;
}
}
```

The *set()* function allows us to assign data. Except for when one single variable is passed to the view (for example, an array containing all of the data to be formatted as JSON), the derived classes will need to overload this parameter. The same is true for the *send()* function, which launches the process of sending the information to the browser. The *encodehtml()* function is the recursive function we used earlier to protect against XSS attacks (see section 4.2.3): it encodes characters such as <, >, &, and quotes before sending them to the browser to be processed by the browser's HTML interpreter.

Below, we show how to write a *ViewJsonAjax* class, which will be dedicated to sending JSON-formatted data in response to an AJAX request:

```
class ViewJsonAjax extends View {
   function send($param = "") {
      /*
       * Encode the data
       */
      $data = array ();
      foreach ( $this->data as $key => $value )
         $data [$key] = $this->encodehtml ( $value
            );
         /*
       * Send to the browser
       */
      ob_clean ();
      echo json_encode ( $data );
      ob_flush ();
   }
}
```

The *send()* function is the only one that needs to be specifically coded. Before converting the array into JSON, its content is transcoded to avoid possible XSS attacks. The file is then sent to the browser, after emptying the PHP cache (*ob_clean()* command).

If other encodings are required, adding them to these classes will make them available throughout the whole application.

6.2.3. *Controller*

The controller plays an essential role: it decides whether or not the requested module can be executed. It must verify that the user has the correct permissions to perform the requested operations.

It is also responsible for cleaning data provided as input (checking UTF-8 encoding, for example – see section 4.3.1). Depending on the result obtained after executing a module, it will call other modules, if necessary. For example, after one module performs a write operation, the controller subsequently calls another module to display a new page in the browser.

Finally, once all of the operations have been completed, it asks the view to launch the process of sending information to the browser. All of these tasks can be summarized as in Figure 6.3.

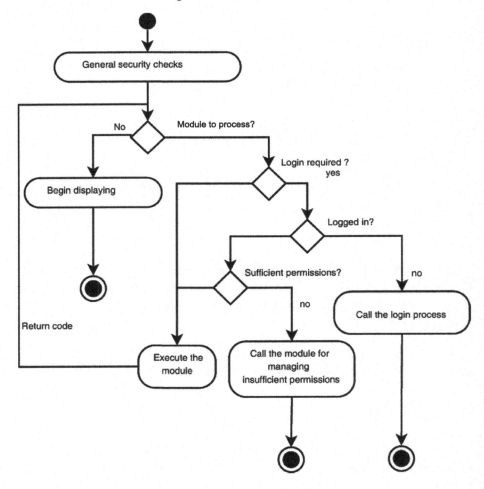

Figure 6.3. *General diagram of the principle of the controller*

The controller first performs various security checks, such as verifying the UTF-8 encoding, inspecting the IP address, etc. If the requested modules require the user to be logged in, but this has not yet been performed, it will redirect the user to the login module.

Executing a module might require specific permissions, which will be verified by the controller. Additional storyboard checks may be necessary to ensure that writing a record to the database only happens after an input form is displayed (not shown in the diagram).

After executing a module, and depending on the code returned, the controller can choose to execute other modules. As we have seen, this is typically what happens when processing a form: the application will need to subsequently display the result or return to a list of folders, and this display process is generally described by dedicated modules.

Finally, the script ends by asking the view to begin displaying.

6.2.3.1. *Linked controllers*

We considered the relatively simple example (but sufficient for most web applications) of an application with a single controller that handles everything.

In other languages, such as Java, there are specialized controllers dedicated to operating the objects associated with them. They can communicate with each other using observation mechanisms (controllers register with other controllers, and each controller informs the list of registered controllers whenever an action is performed).

It is important to ensure that controllers are only listened to by one other controller at any given time, following a tree-like structure as shown in Figure 6.4. We should avoid having connections in all directions (sometimes described as *spaghetti code*). This guarantees that we will be able to maintain the code in the long term, since the path is relatively simple to reconstruct.

This approach is often implemented by "client-heavy" applications written in Java.

The main controller receives information from specialized controllers, typically one controller per input module (these modules can optionally be declared in separate windows). Each component in the window, such as the menu, can also be operated by its own controller.

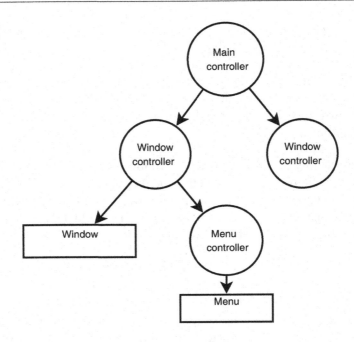

Figure 6.4. *Linked controllers*

If a piece of information from one window needs to be passed to another, the entire chain of controllers is responsible for transmitting the message: this guarantees that the message will only be processed once, and makes the code more reusable. Adding or deleting a window does not undermine the overall architecture.

6.2.3.2. *Inherited controllers*

Most professional frameworks use inherited controllers. To execute a module, a controller is created from a single class containing the basic code. To make this controller operational, we simply need to specify the permissions assigned to it, the view that it generates, etc.

This is in fact the principle used by Symphony (a PHP programming framework widely used in professional circles [SYM 15]). The controller, part of the model, and part of the view (as presented above) are merged together: there is one controller for each module and page that can be executed.

All of these controllers inherit from an underlying object that already contains the mechanisms required to manage permissions, login and operation sequences (handover of control to another controller after execution). The main drawback of this approach is that it is difficult to quickly visualize the overall architecture of the application, and modifying its structure or permissions management can be more difficult: these aspects are defined within each controller, and not at a single location.

6.2.3.3. *Single-object controllers*

In environments that handle very intensive graphical processes, such as drawing software, some controllers will monitor the modifications made to a single graphical component in real time. Each graphical object is thus associated with a controller that is activated every time that an action is performed. This action is then propagated to all other listening controllers, which will trigger state changes in all objects associated with one of them.

Thus, modifying any field in a form will immediately prompt the controller to detect the new input value and send it to the database management handler (ORM).

This approach is much more reactive than the one typically used in web environments, where information is only taken into account when the user validates it, for example by clicking on a "submit" button. However, it can be more difficult to implement if certain actions need to know the state of multiple other components.

6.3. Conclusion

We have seen that the MVC model allows the entire application code to be more easily protected by guaranteeing that all information is processed consistently.

For novice developers, working with the MVC model can be somewhat unsettling. Indeed, before any information can be displayed, and thus before any operations can be tested, a number of suitable lines of code need to be written throughout all compartments of the model (the view, the model management class(es) and the controller). This requires a certain level of abstraction that can be difficult to achieve while simultaneously learning other aspects relating to programming practice and the programming language.

Even though writing the first module can be a laborious process, the effort invested in learning the MVC model will yield ample returns by making subsequent modules easier to write, easier to maintain, and by providing a global overview of the application.

From the perspective of security, using this design approach (or another equivalent approach) is essentially mandatory to guarantee a consistent level of security throughout the development process and successive versions of the application.

7

Implementing a Suitable Technical Platform and Testing the Application

7.1. Designing a suitable technical architecture

7.1.1. *Integrating security into the earliest stages of the project*

Security is a highly structural aspect of applications. If not built into the project right from the start, it can be difficult to implement *a posteriori*. Ensuring that variables are properly typed and that all pages are processed uniformly without omitting any of the required checks is relatively easy when planned from the beginning. Attempting to do this later means combing through the code, which quickly becomes tedious, and poorly designed or unsuitable architectures can be expensive to modify. Structured approaches like the MVC approach (model – view – controller (see Chapter 6)) are therefore highly beneficial.

Software is never intrinsically secure: the execution environment of an application, consisting of the servers and networks that host it and the mechanisms for monitoring infrastructure and attempted intrusions, plays a key role in the application security level.

But security is not an end unto itself: it can be expensive to implement and should be proportionate to the risks posed by the application from the perspective of the company developing it. Risk analysis is an essential step and should be conducted at the earliest stages of the project. In some cases, the conclusions of risk analysis will prompt us to choose special development architectures to ensure that data and access are properly protected. In extreme cases, the risks associated with the project brought to light by this analysis can force the project to be abandoned, since the potential benefits do not justify the risks.

Finally, we should avoid overconfidence and always keep one ear to the ground for new developments: each generation of hackers is more curious than the last. A successful attack can quickly transform arrogance into humility.

All applications in production require regular security inspections and must be kept up-to-date with technical developments so that additional protections can quickly be integrated if a new type of risk surfaces. An application viewed as secure today may not be in 5 years' time.

7.1.2. *Using code management systems such as GIT*

When a small company feels the need to develop software, the developer often sets up a simple platform consisting of a web server and a database. The program is written directly onto the web server, and as soon as an operational version is available, access is opened to users.

Changes are made "on the fly", directly to the application. Conscientious developers might plan different versions of the application and separate databases for testing and production, but everything will nonetheless be hosted on the same platform.

This architecture will eventually reach its limits: an accidental modification can disrupt the production software, a poorly programmed loop that fails to terminate (infinite loop) or a badly designed SQL query can jeopardize the server resources and hinder access to the program.

Code management tools such as GIT [SCM 15] can be used to track all changes made to the application. These changes can be published in a repository, either a private repository on a platform created using GITLAB [GIT 16b], for example, or a public repository such as GITHUB [GIT 16a]. It is easy to generate the application code from these repositories: this makes it very straightforward to separate development platforms from production platforms.

However, some precautions are necessary when using GIT. The *.git* folder, created in the project root directory, should not be uploaded to the production website: it contains a copy of all generated code. Similarly, we should avoid storing any files containing database access information in GIT to prevent anybody from finding them later. This can be done by adding a few commands to the GIT exclusions file, *.gitignore*, placed in the root directory of the repository:

```
# text editor save files
*~
# file containing connection details
param.inc.php
# folder containing temporary files generated by
   the application
temp/
```

GIT also allows multiple developers to work together by generating multiple branches, which makes it easier to develop multiple versions of the application and manage updates and patches.

7.1.3. *Using software to design the database*

SQL uses commands to create tables and other objects. In the design phases of a project, it is often more convenient to use graphical tools to design the tables and the relations between them.

Once the database structure has been designed, these tools generate SQL scripts that apply the corresponding changes to the model of an existing database. Most of these tools store a representation of the database in an XML file that might be archived and subject to GIT version control.

Personally, I have used SQL Architect [SOF 16] for many years. This software supports most types of database engine. Although it has a few shortcomings, it is simple and easy to implement.

7.1.4. Implementing separate architectures for development and production

In the previous chapters, we saw that it is essential to use different accounts to access the development and production databases. PostgreSQL, for example, restricts certain accounts using IP filtering so that they can only log in from certain machines (see section 4.3.4). If all databases are hosted on the same platform, this precaution does not help.

GIT and database modeling tools make it easy to separate development platforms from production platforms. This prevents issues when writing the code by avoiding the risk of accidentally modifying the production data, or negatively affecting the performance of the live application.

To limit the risks of incidents when the application is pushed into production, most large companies typically set up one or several preproduction platforms, which are identical copies of the production platform. All updates are first applied to these platforms, and if everything is found to be satisfactory after testing, the update is then carried over to the final platform.

Figure 7.1 gives one example of the platforms that could be implemented.

The developers work on their own computers, which have built-in web servers for testing the code, and databases that can be manipulated as much as necessary.

All changes are stored on the GIT server. When a version of the application is ready for testing, it is installed on the test platform, which has a web server and a database.

Once this version is ready for production, it is first installed on the preproduction platform. All functional tests are repeated to verify that everything works properly. This platform can also be used to test the production launch phase, for example by checking the scripts that apply changes to the database.

Finally, once everything is working as expected, the new version is pushed to the production platform.

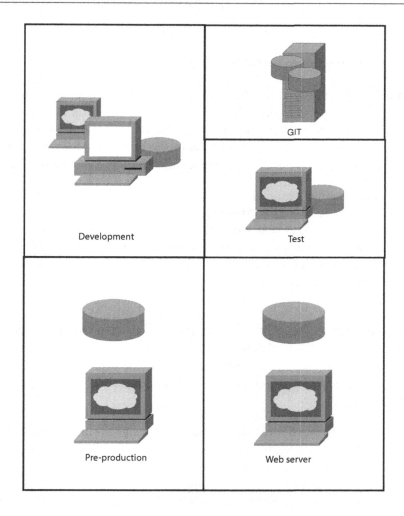

Figure 7.1. *Example of one possible arrangement
of technical platforms*

Another possibility that we have not yet mentioned is to include an additional platform for testing the security of the application (see below).

The procedures for launching a new version of the application into production are often documented by implementing special processes, typically based on ITIL [WIK 15d], a collection of good practices for IT production management.

7.2. Testing the security of the application

7.2.1. *Analyzing vulnerabilities with ZAP Proxy*

Attackers often use automatic mechanisms to discover vulnerabilities: to find a security hole, they launch a comprehensive range of tests that make it easier for them to identify any mistakes that the programmers might have made. They usually begin by mapping the file system to find folders that might allow them to access either administrative modules or hidden information.

To ensure that our application is secure, we need to be at least as thorough as the attackers. Following a tried-and-tested approach is essential. Keeping up-to-date with IT news and knowing a few common vulnerabilities is not enough to be safe: how can programmers be sure that they know every possible kind of attack? Even if they do, how can they be sure that the protective measures included in the code are working properly? How can they check whether anything was forgotten?

Projects such as the ASVS by OWASP, which we discussed earlier (see section 2.5.1), publish checklists of tests that should be performed before each update is applied to the production platform. These tests allow us to ensure that the most frequent types of attack have been properly accounted for during development.

However, this is still not sufficient. Just because we believe that our software is protected does not mean that it is true. One simple oversight, one small instance of carelessness when writing a module can open a vulnerability that attackers can exploit. Intrusion tests are necessary to ensure that the protective measures are actually effective.

In recent months, I have been testing my applications with the tool *ZAP Proxy* [OWA 15b], which we will discuss below. All of my applications are built according to the same model, and the last few times that I tested them with this tool, it did not find any significant flaws.

When I wrote my last application, I felt confident in the work that I had done, and I considered skipping the penetration test. Intrusion testing is admittedly a somewhat cumbersome process, and requires a specially implemented platform to avoid corrupting the database or production databases, among other things. I ultimately decided to dedicate a few hours to running the test anyway, and it is a good thing I did: one of the configuration files contained a mistake, and an "SQL injection" vulnerability (see section 4.2.1) was found.

Furthermore, risks change over time. Software that was considered to be relatively secure a decade ago probably would not be today: it is essential to regularly browse specialized websites to check that no new attack scenarios have been developed. Repeating penetration testing at regular intervals, between 3 and 5 years for low-priority applications, and yearly for high-stakes applications, is probably advisable.

The ZAP Proxy program was written in Java, and is based on the Eclipse RCP[1] (Rich Client Platform) [ECL 14].

It has two main modes of operation.

The first mode allows us to listen to all of the information passed between the browser and the website (or web application) and analyze it. This allows us to inspect cookies, small files used to store information in the browser, as well as the way that sessions are implemented. It can also record all of the pages that were viewed, for purposes of analysis or to mount an attack.

To listen to these communications, ZAP Proxy places itself between the web server and the browser, similar to a man-in-the-middle attack [WIK 15a]. To activate this mode, the browser must be manually configured to use a proxy server at the ZAP Proxy listening port, the port 8080 (see Figure 7.2).

ZAP intercepts everything passed between the browser and the web server. It can handle HTTPS-encrypted connections: it presents a certificate to the browser, decrypts the communication and then re-encrypts it to send it to the server. It performs the reverse operation with information sent by the application.

---

1 Eclipse is a software development suite originally designed for writing Java programs, but which has since been extended to support many other languages. The engine that drives it has a number of extremely useful general-purpose features, such as file system management, primary and auxiliary window control, etc. The rich functionality of its interface and the ability to install plugins have made it a popular choice for developing a wide range of applications: since the graphical layer already works, programmers can focus on developing technical content. Applications based on this platform all have the same overall appearance, which additionally makes them easier to learn for users.

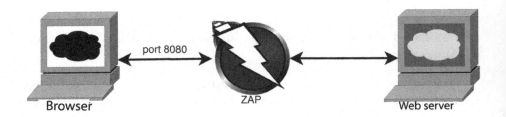

Figure 7.2. *Principle of ZAP Proxy*

This allows it to record and analyze everything without changing anything: this is the passive, non-destructive mode.

The second mode is attack mode. It has two main modules: the first finds all accessible files and webpages on the site, and the second attempts to find security holes by launching attack scenarios.

In this mode, positioning the program between the browser and the application is no longer required: it can send requests directly to the server.

This mode is dangerous: the software will attempt to write information to the database to demonstrate that an exploit (a potentially successful attack) exists. It requires a few precautions, especially for the database. Once the test has been performed, the database will be unusable, and will need to be destroyed.

Since this software generates actual attacks, it should never be used against a website that you do not own: doing so would be a reprehensible act.

Some preparation is required before launching a penetration test. The following operations need to be performed:

7.2.1.1. *Implement a test platform*

The platform must be as close as possible to the platform used for production. It should have a copy of the database, with the same versions for the web server, the same configuration for encryption, etc.

The information in the database will be corrupted by the penetration test: it is absolutely essential to ensure that we are working with a copy of the database that can freely be deleted afterward.

To avoid problems, always review the settings of the application hosted on this platform. In particular, always check that the database that you are using is the one prepared specifically for this purpose: a mistake in a variable can cause significant damage.

7.2.1.2. *Configure the browser*

If possible, use a browser dedicated specifically to security testing. You can also manage several profiles. For example, with Firefox [MOZ 16a], you can create new profiles or select them by adding the *-P* option to the launch command.

Configure the browser settings to use the proxy with address: *localhost:8080*. Port 8080 is used by ZAP to listen to and intercept communications.

7.2.1.3. *Begin automatic file system discovery*

In ZAP, in the menu, select *Tools > Spider...* (or press *Crtl-Alt-S*). Enter the address of your application, e.g. *http://localhost/myapp*.

The program will immediately start searching for accessible pages and will conduct an initial analysis. In the Alerts tab, you can see the potential issues detected by the program, usually resulting from improperly implemented protocols (for example, protective measures in the browser that have not been activated).

You can also view the file system tree that the program was able to detect. If some folders that were not supposed to be accessible were discovered, one of the protections must be poorly configured.

7.2.1.4. *Browsing the application*

After configuring your browser to allow ZAP Proxy to listen, connect your application with an account specially set aside for this purpose.

This account must have full permissions (you can also repeat the tests with reduced permissions to check the robustness of the permissions management system). Ideally, it should be stored locally: if it is ever deleted by the tests or locked (passwords changed and tested), this will make it easier to reset.

Complete each screen and perform each operation offered by the application: the more exhaustive you make this process, the more comprehensive the testing will be.

All of the visited pages (links) will appear in the file tree.

7.2.1.5. *Disable the attack on login and logout pages*

Unless you specifically wish to test the login pages, it is a good idea to configure ZAP Proxy to skip testing them. Indeed, it will attempt to fill the fields with special values to test for exploits, including the password fields. This can cause your password to be locked and can cause subsequent tests to fail, since the user will not be logged in.

Find the login and logout pages in the file tree, and configure ZAP Proxy to remove them from the attack (right-click on each URL, *exclude from > Scanner*).

7.2.1.6. *Launch the attack*

In the file tree, *right-click* on your application root directory and select *Attack > Active Scan....* The program will launch attacks on each of the pages listed.

When the attack scenarios are executed, several thousands of tests will be performed. This takes time. Even on a powerful computer, it can take dozens of minutes to generate the results.

7.2.1.7. *Analyzing the results*

Locate the anomalies detected by the program. Correct the code and then repeat all tests. Remember in particular to reload a clean copy of the database, since the previous attack will have written information to the database to test it for vulnerabilities.

When this kind of study is performed, it often takes several "flaw discovery/correction" cycles to obtain clean code.

Performing quick scans on portions of code after they are written can also be a good idea, to avoid having to go over everything just before production.

This analysis should therefore be performed after completing each major module of the application to verify that it has been properly coded. Similarly,

ZAP Proxy changes over time, as new tests are added: repeating the global tests at regular intervals is always beneficial.

Once all of the tests have passed, repeating any failed tests until each of the detected security issues is resolved, and the documents have been validated, you can enjoy the satisfaction of knowing that the development of your application is finally complete. Although there is still no guarantee that attackers will not be able to penetrate the application, you will have at least made their life difficult, and tightened the security of the immaterial capital of your company or your customers.

7.2.2. *Certifying the application*

Doing tests is good, but proving that they have been done is better.

Security documents should be compiled detailing each of the tasks performed: the analysis of the risks posed by the application, the definitions of the required security levels, the description of the choice of methodology (selection of ASVS standard level, test protocol) and the results obtained. Some tests may return positive: there may be reasons that justify these results, but if so explanations should be given.

7.2.3. *Write the implementation documents*

We saw earlier that software cannot be intrinsically secure: the way that it is implemented within the server plays a major role in its overall security. The web server configuration parameters will likely need to be adjusted to force the server to operate more securely than it does by default. Some other changes might also need to be applied to the application itself (adapting a configuration file, deleting unused accounts after installation, etc.). These operations need to be specified to the team responsible for implementing the application.

The best way of doing this is to write a document detailing the expected implementation constraints chosen during development. This document should state the required web server configuration, the location of specific folders if necessary, the accounts that should be deleted after installation, etc.

These documents will make it easier for the software requester to have it validated. It might be necessary to have the application validated by an authority: for example, this is mandatory for web applications developed by the French government. The documents will support the approval process.

Once the software is in production, the team responsible for its operation will need to ensure that the implemented configuration is consistent with the stated requirements at regular intervals. Changes that influence the behavior or the security of the application can accrue over time.

7.3. What options do we have if implementing security measures for an application seems an impossible task?

We are nearing the end of this book. It might be the case that securing an application would require more skills or time resources than are available for the project, but that there is nonetheless a pressing need for automation, and choosing not to develop an application would therefore represent an inappropriate or counter-productive solution.

What should we do in this situation? Is compiling specifications and outsourcing the development to another company the right solution? This is probably ideal, but writing these specifications can be complicated.

The first step is the unavoidable process of defining the security needs, i.e. the consequences of a breach of integrity, availability or confidentiality in the prospective application. This step is not particularly complex and does not require any specialized computer skills, only common sense. Besides, as we remarked earlier (see section 2.6), defining these risks is not the responsibility of the developers, as they do not manage the business aspects and related issues.

But the question of the specifications remains to be resolved.

In industrial contexts, writing the specifications to manufacture a part is a relatively straightforward process. We proceed by defining the material, specifying the dimensions, indicating the number of components to be manufactured, the technical constraints that must be observed, etc. After a call for tenders, the contractor delivers a prototype batch that can be inspected before manufacturing the final order. The software industry has attempted to copy this approach with the so-called V-model [WIK 15b].

The major issue with this approach is that creating software is first and foremost an intellectual activity, and that attempting to predict the details of the working product in advance is extremely difficult. Ideas only materialize and the needs are only identified during writing and testing. Compiling the specifications for software is often a difficult operation that requires heavy time investment, either from the users (project management support) or the IT specialists who help to shape the requirements. A new profession was in fact born to accomplish this task, *project management assistance*, which is responsible for transcribing the needs expressed by the future users in terms that can be understood by the developers.

Writing the specifications is a lengthy process, and it can be months or even years between the start of writing and delivery. By this point, the requirements will likely have changed, for example because of advancements in the state of technology, or because the application that was originally planned is no longer useful by the time it is ready.

To overcome these problems, new techniques were designed in the early 2000s, such as agile methods inspired by the Agile Manifesto [BEC 01], requiring far lighter specifications. Although these approaches are effective, they require the software requester to be present during the development phase, which might create conflicts in scheduling or in the availability of resources.

To overcome these constraints, an interesting approach has begun to emerge in the field of scientific research.

Some researchers with basic knowledge of programming have designed programs to perform the operations that they need. These programs might, for example, take the form of a spreadsheet, with more or less extensive use of macros and calculation functions.

From the perspective of IT, these programs are highly flawed: redundant code, no security measures, lack of user-friendliness, complicated to update, etc. But this work nonetheless provides a working model: by analyzing it, it is easy to find the computational principles, the features that are either expected or already implemented, etc. For a developer, this is much better than a set of specifications: it provides a working demonstration of the expectations of the party requesting the application. Using their own tools, developers can then create an application to meet these needs subject to professional standards and including all necessary security measures.

Returning to our original question, if a user wants to create a tool for personal use, but feels overwhelmed either technically or due to time commitments, he/she can simply create his/her own program. The requirements can be refined as the program is developed. Once the product is sufficiently mature, it can be handed over to an IT professional or service company. The model will make it easy to create software that complies with modern standards. The specifications will be much easier to write: the service provided will simply be to format an application based on previously performed work. To ensure that security is properly taken into consideration, a risk assessment must be provided and the required level of security must be defined.

The work that has already been performed will not be lost, and everybody benefits: the party requesting the application can be sure that the software will properly meet its needs and will be implemented according to modern development and security standards, and the developers will have a reference model that they can use to build the application.

Bibliography

[ANS 10] ANSSI, "EBIOS – Expression des Besoins et Identification des Objectifs de Sécurité", available at: http://www.ssi.gouv.fr/administration/guide/ebios-2010-expression-des-besoins-et-identification-des-objectifs-de-securite, 2010.

[ANS 13] ANSSI, "Recommandations pour la sécurisation des sites web", available at: http://www.ssi.gouv.fr/uploads/IMG/pdf/NPSecuriteWebNoteTech.pdf, 2013.

[ANS 14] ANSSI, "Référentiel général de sécurité, annexe B1, version 2.03", available at: http://www.ssi.gouv.fr/uploads/2015/01/RGSv-2-0B1.pdf, 2014.

[ANS 15] ANSSI, "Site institutionnel", available at: http://www.ssi.gouv.fr/, 2015.

[APA 16] APACHE, "HTTP server project", available at: https://apache.org, 2016.

[BEC 01] BECK K., BEEDLE M., VAN BENNEKUM A. et al., "Le manifeste Agile", available at: http://agilemanifesto.org/iso/fr/, 2001.

[BEN 10] BENILLOUCHE J., "Comment le virus Stuxnet s'en est pris au programme nucléaire iranien", available at: http://www.slate.fr/story/30471/stuxnet-virus-programme-nucleaire-iranien, 2010.

[CLA 15a] CLAMAV, "Clamav", available at: https://wiki.archlinux.org/index.php/ClamAV, 2015.

[CLA 15b] CLAMAV, "Site officiel", available at: http://www.clamav.net/, 2015.

[CLU 15a] CLUSIF, "Page d'accueil de Méhari", available at: https://clusif.fr/fr/production/mehari/presentation.asp, 2015 .

[CLU 15b] CLUSIF, "Site officiel", available at: http://www.clusif.asso.fr/, 2015.

[COB 16] COBUCCI L.O., "A simple library to work with JSON web token and JSON Web Signature", available at: https://github.com/lcobucci/jwt, 2016.

[DIG 15] DIGITALOCEAN, "How To Set Up mod_security with Apache on Debian/Ubuntu", available at: https://www.digitalocean.com/community/tutorials/how-to-set-up-modsecurity-with-apache-on-debian-ubuntu, 2015.

[ECL 14] ECLIPSE FOUNDATION, "Rich Client Platform", available at: http://wiki.eclipse.org/ index.php/RichClientPlatform, 2014.

[ELS 15] VAN ELST R., "Strong SSL Security on Apache2", available at: https://raymii.org/ s/tutorials/StrongSSLSecurityOnApache2.html, 2015.

[GIT 16a] GITHUB, "How people build software", available at: https://github.com, 2016.

[GIT 16b] GITLAB, "Coder, tester, et déployer ensemble", available at: https://about. gitlab.com, 2016.

[ISO 09] ISO, "ISO 31000:2009", available at: http://www.iso.org/iso/fr/home/store/ cataloguetc/cataloguedetail.htm?csnumber=43170, 2009.

[ISO 11] ISO, "ISO/IEC 27005:2011", available at: http://www.iso.org/iso/fr/home/store/ cataloguetc/cataloguedetail.htm?csnumber=56742, 2011.

[ISO 15] ISO, "ISO/IEC 27001 - Management de la sécurité de l'information", available at: http://www.iso.org/iso/fr/home/standards/management-standards/iso27001.htm, 2015.

[ITE 15] ITESPRESSO, "Vol massif de données : les membres d'AdultFriendFinder.com mis à nu à leur insu", available at: http://www.itespresso.fr/vol-massif-donnees-membres-adultfriendfinder-com-mis-a-nu-insu-96763.html, 2015.

[JAS 15] JASIG, "PHPCAS", available at: https://wiki.jasig.org/display/CASC/phpCAS, 2015.

[JQU 15] JQUERY, "Site officiel", available at: http://jquery.com/, 2015.

[JWT 16] JWT, "JSON Web Tokens", available at: http://jwt.io, 2016.

[LAB 16] LABS Q.S., "SSL Server Test", available at: https://www.ssllabs.com/ssltest, 2016.

[LEI 13] LEIRN, "Pure PHP Syslog Class", available at: https://github.com/ leirn/php.syslog.class, 2013.

[LEM 14] LEMONDE, "Vol massif de données bancaires en Corée du Sud", available at: http://www.lemonde.fr/economie/article/2014/01/22/vol-massif-de-donnees-bancaires-en-coree-du-sud43523133234.html, 2014.

[MIC 16] MICROSOFT, "A flexible and easy-to-manage web server...", available at: http://www.iis.net, 2016.

[MOD 15] MODSECURITY, "Mod_security, site officiel", available at: http://www. modsecurity.org/, 2015.

[MOZ 15] MOZILLA FOUNDATION, "Thunderbird, un logiciel pour rendre votre messagerie plus facile", available at: https://www.mozilla.org/fr/thunderbird/, 2015.

[MOZ 16a] MOZILLA, "Firefox", available at: https://www.mozilla.org/fr/firefox/new/, 2016.

[MOZ 16b] MOZILLA, "Mozilla SSL Configuration Generator", available at: https://mozilla.github.io/server-side-tls/ssl-config-generator/, 2016.

[NET 16] NETCRAFT, "Web Server Survey", available at: http://news.netcraft.com/ archives/2016/02/22/february-2016-web-server-survey.html, 2016.

[NGI 16] NGINX, "NGINX", available at: http://nginx.org, 2016.

[NOT 15] NOTAIRES DE FRANCE, "Signer un acte authentique électronique", available at: http://www.notaires.fr/fr/lettre-notaires-france/signer-un-acte-authentique-électronique, 2015.

[OAU 16] OAUTH, "OAuth community site", available at: http://oauth.net, 2016.

[OPE 15] OPENLDAP, "Site officiel", available at: https://wiki.jasig.org/display/CASC/phpCAS, 2015.

[OWA 13] OWASP, "Top 10 2013", available at: http://owosp.org/index.php/Top_10_2013-Top_10, 2013.

[OWA 14a] OWASP, "Application security verification standard (2014)", available at: https://www.owasp.org/images/5/58/OWASPASVSVersion2.pdf, 2014.

[OWA 14b] OWASP, "Exigences de sécurité – fichier Excel en français", available at: https://www.owasp.org/images/8/89/Asvsv2itemsfr.xlsx, 2014.

[OWA 14c] OWASP, "Testing for XML Injection (OTG-INPVAL-008)", available at: https://www.owasp.org/index.php/XPATHInjection, 2014.

[OWA 15a] OWASP, "Site institutionnel", available at: https://www.owasp.org, 2015.

[OWA 15b] OWASP, "Zed Attack Proxy Project", available at: https://www.owasp.org/index.php/OWASP_Zed_Attack_Proxy_Project, 2015.

[PGA 14] PGADMIN, "PgAdmin – PostgreSql Tools", available at: http://www.pgadmin.org, 2014.

[PHP 06] PHPGACL, "phpGACL", available at: http://sourceforge.net/projects/phpgacl/, 2006.

[QUI 12] QUINTON E., "Mettre en place un serveur central de logs avec Rsyslog", available at: http://www.linux-professionnel.net/securite/mettre-en-place-un-serveur-central-de-logs- avec-rsyslog, 2012.

[QUI 16] QUINTON E., "Tableau des exigences ASVS en français", available at: http://www.linux-professionnel.net/securite/asvs-v3-items-fr/asvsv3itemsfr.ods, 2016.

[RSY 16] RSYSLOG, "Rsyslog, the rocket-fast system for log processing", available at: http://www.rsyslog.com, 2016.

[SCM 15] GIT SCM, "Git –everything-is-local", available at: http://git-scm.com/, 2015.

[SHI 16] SHIBBOLETH, "shibboleth", available at: https://shibboleth.net, 2016.

[SMA 16] SMARTY, "Smarty, PHP Template Engine", available at: http://www.smarty.net, 2016.

[SOF 16] SOFTWARE S.P., "Data Modeling & Profiling Tool : SQL Power Architect", available at: http://www.sqlpower.ca, 2016.

[SOU 14] SOURCEFORGE, "Php-Clamav", available at: http://sourceforge.net/projects/php-clamav/, 2014.

[SYM 15] SYMPHONY, "Symphony - site officiel", available at: http://symfony.com/, 2015.

[TUX 11] TUXPLANET, "Installation et configuration de Mod_security", available at: http://www.tux-planet.fr/installation-et-configuration-de-modsecurity/, 2011.

[WAP 15] WAPPALYZER, "Site officiel", available at: https://wappalyzer.com/, 2015.

[WIK 15a] WIKIPEDIA, "Attaque de l'homme du milieu", available at: https://fr.wikipedia.org/wiki/Attaquedel'hommedumilieu, 2015.

[WIK 15b] WIKIPEDIA, "Cycle en V", available at: https://fr.wikipedia.org/wiki/CycleenV, 2015.

[WIK 15c] WIKIPEDIA, "DigiNotar", available at: https://en.wikipedia.org/wiki/DigiNotar, 2015.

[WIK 15d] WIKIPEDIA, "ITIL", available at: https://en.wikipedia.org/wiki/ITIL, 2015.

[WIK 15e] WIKIPEDIA, "Lightweight directory access protocol", available at: https://fr.wikipedia.org/wiki/LightweightDirectoryAccessProtocol, 2015.

[WIK 15f] WIKIPEDIA, "List of HTTP status codes", available at: https://en.wikipedia.org/wiki/ListofHTTPstatuscodes, 2015.

[WIK 15g] WIKIPEDIA, "Loi de Moore", available at: https://fr.wikipedia.org/wiki/LoideMoore, 2015.

[WIK 15h] WIKIPEDIA, "Transport layer security", available at: https://fr.wikipedia.org/wiki/TransportLayerSecurity, 2015.

[WIK 16a] WIKIPEDIA, "Computer emergency response team", available at: https://fr.wikipedia.org/ wiki/ComputerEmergencyResponseTeam, 2016.

[WIK 16b] WIKIPEDIA, "Object-relational mapping", available at: https://en.wikipedia.org/wiki/Object-relationalmapping, 2016.

[WIK 16c] WIKIPEDIA, "Type MIME", available at: https://fr.wikipedia.org/wiki/TypeMIME, 2016.

[WOR 15] WORDPRESS, "Wordpress francophone – site institutionnel", available at: http://www.wordpress-fr.net/, 2015.

[ZDN 14] ZDNET, "Une faille critique dévoilée dans WordPress", available at: http://www.zdnet.fr/actualites/une-faille-critique-devoilee-dans-wordpress-39810019.htm, 2014.

Index

Printed in the United States
By Bookmasters